JN087470

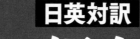

日英対訳

世界に紹介したい日本の100人

ジェームス・M・バーダマン [著]
James M. Vardaman

長尾実佐子 [訳]
Nagao Misako

Introducing
100 Impressive
Japanese

山川出版社

はじめに

Preface

日本に初めて来た頃、自分が目にするほぼあらゆるものに魅了されました。日本人のことや何世代にもわたって受け継がれてきた習慣について、英語で書かれた本で読めば読むほど、興味をかき立てられたものです。

　私の場合はありがたいことに、目にするものや事の次第、日本という国の発展や変遷について英語で教えてくれる人々に出会えましたが、私が日本に来てから友人になった人々は、そうした物事の説明の仕方を知らないこともあれば、私のような欧米出身者が日本に興味を持つようになるとは思いもしないということがありました。彼らが違う視点から日本を見るようになったのは、私の好奇心に背中を押されてのことだったのです。

　本書の目的は、さまざまな時代に日本人が成し遂げた偉業に興味を持ってもらうことにあります。掲載されている100人は、何らかの形で現代の日本につながるこの国の発展にさまざまな形で大いに貢献したという私なりの考えで選んでいます。

　この100人は創意工夫を凝らして世に革新をもたらし、日本人の生活様式や考え方、時には日本以外の国々にも影響を与えた人物で、芸術家、科学者、実業家、技術者、政治家、哲学者、神学者、音楽家、経済学者など多岐にわたります。ご自分の好きな日本人が入っていなかったら申し訳ないのですが、時代や専門性のバランスを考慮して選んでみました。

　私がこの100人を重要だと考える理由の一つは、彼ら彼女らがそれまでの考え方を根本から変え、後世に影響を与えたためです。もう一つの理由として、彼ら彼女らには優れた協力者がおり、他者から得た適切な材料、道具、技術、技能を備えていたことが挙げられます。例えば、芸術家は技能やテーマ、素材などを先人から学び、実業家は技術、資金源、労働力、そして自分が生産したものを歓迎してくれる市場を受け継いでいるのです。

　この100人が日本の歴史で最も重要な人物だから挙げていると思われる

のは私の本意ではありません。本書の目的は、この100人について百科事典に載っているような詳細を論じることではなく、日本人以外の人々にこの100人の業績を英語で説明するときの表現方法を学んでもらうことにあります。そのため、なぜ、彼ら彼女らは重要な存在だったのか、どんなことで社会に貢献したのか、そうした点を挙げながら、日本の伝統について説明することを心掛けました。

　人物紹介は対訳形式になっており、一つの節は簡潔かつ情報量が多い中級レベルの英語で、1項目は250ワード前後です。語注付きなので、あまり辞書を引かなくても話が理解できるようになっています。英語が最初は理解できなくても、読み直して基本的な内容を把握してみてください。一字一句理解しようとする必要はありません。

　日本語訳は補助的なもので、逐語訳や直訳は意図していません。英文の内容を理解しやすいように、日本の歴史的な用語や記述の形式に合わせて、適宜意訳や言い換えをしています。外国の人たちに理解してもらうための簡潔な英語の記述を、分かりやすい日本語に移し替えることは異文化コミュニケーションの一つの試みでもあるのです。

　この場を借りて、翻訳を担当してくれた長尾実佐子氏にお礼を申し上げます。また、この企画を完成にまで導いてくれた細田繁氏に心から感謝申し上げます。

　最後に、読者の皆様には、本書に掲載された100人の日本人を世界に紹介する方法を学んでもらい、場合によっては、自分の先人たちについて、もっと知りたいと思うようになってもらえれば、著者としてこれほど嬉しいことはありません。日本は大変興味深く面白い国です。日本人以外の人々に日本人のことを知る手助けをしていただければ幸いです。

2021年　ジェームス・M・バーダマン

目次 Contents

Chapter 3 近代・現代 Modern Period／Contemporary Period

参考文献 References

■英文は各人物のエッセンスを紹介するためシンプルな記述となっていますが、
和文ではより分かりやすくするために英文にない事柄も（　）で補っています。

■英文の赤字の語句は、語注にその辞書的な一般的な訳語を載せています。
和文の赤字は英文の赤字語句におよそ対応するところを赤字にしていますが、
日本の歴史用語や文脈に合わせて意訳している部分では完全に対応していない場合もあります。

■英文の末尾にテキストのワード数を載せています。
英文読解スピードの参考にしてください。

Chapter 1 ──────
古代・中世
Ancient Period／Medieval Period

Kakinomoto no Hitomaro

Empress Komyo

Emperor Kanmu

Shotoku Taishi

Ono no Komachi

Saigyo

Honen

Unkei

Oda Nobunaga

Kamo no Chomei

Minamoto no Yoshitsune

Sen no Rikyu

Hojo Masako

Emperor Go-Daigo

Hosokawa Gracia

01 Himiko
Legendary Queen of Wa

A third-century history of the **Wei dynasty** of China compiled by a man who died in 297 A.D. mentions a kingdom in the Japanese islands. Called Yamatai, the kingdom is described as having more than 70,000 **households** and being ruled by **hereditary** kings and queens. The Chinese history in the section dealing with Japan, calls it the "Land of Wa." And it mentions that conflict broke out among the various "countries" inhabited by the Wa people sometime around late 2nd century.

In particular, the history mentions a woman named Himiko who became a sovereign of the land with the agreement of the **chieftains** of various local groups. Himiko appears to have inspired loyalty because she mastered magic and **sorcery** and it was she who "**bewitched**" the people. She was placed on a **throne**, according to this history, and remained hidden from the people and surrounded by armed guards.

It was once thought that Queen Himiko was a **shaman** who delegated political affairs to a male relative. Perhaps it was a brother who assisted her in actually ruling the country.

More recently, however, scholars have seen the description of her apparently magical powers as simply highlighting the spiritual side of the Japanese **monarch**.

Debate continues not only about Himiko's actual position but also about the location of Yamatai. Whether this **federation** of kingdoms was located in Kyushu or in central Japan remains unclear. It is still unclear whether this Yamatai is distinct from the subsequent Yamato. (245)

卑弥呼

倭国の伝説の女王

［生没年不詳］

　西暦297年に亡くなった男の手による魏王朝の歴史書、『三国志』では、日本列島にあった王国について触れられている。邪馬台国と呼ばれるこの王国は7万戸以上を有し、王や女王が代々統治していた。『三国志』中、日本について述べた巻、「魏志」倭人伝では、日本を「倭国」と呼び、2世紀後半頃に倭人が住むさまざまな「小国」の間で対立が起きたと記している。

　同書が特に言及しているのが、さまざまな集団の長の同意を得て倭国の女王になった卑弥呼だ。卑弥呼は鬼道に長け、人々を「魅了」して人心を掌握していたとされる。同書によれば、卑弥呼は女王になってからは武装した衛兵に囲まれて過ごし、人々の前には姿を現さなかったという。

　卑弥呼について、巫女で、政務は男性の親族に任せ、実際に統治して彼女を補佐していたのは弟ではないかという説もある。

　しかし最近の研究では、卑弥呼が持っていたとされる不思議な力に関する記述は、おそらく日本の君主の精神面を強調するためと考えられている。

　卑弥呼の実際の地位がどのようなものだったのかという謎以外にも、邪馬台国はどこにあったのかという問題に関する論争もいまだ決着がついておらず、この小国連合が九州にあったのか、日本の中央部（近畿）にあったのかはまだ分かっていない。また、邪馬台国は、その後、成立したヤマト王権とは別の国かどうかも謎のままである。

■ Wei dynasty 魏王朝　■ household 世帯　■ hereditary 世襲の　■ chieftain 族長　■ sorcery 黒魔術　■ bewitch 〜の心を奪う　■ throne 王位、皇位　■ shaman 巫女　■ monarch 君主　■ federation 連盟

02 Shotoku Taishi
Introducer of Buddhism

Prince Shotoku, *Shotoku Taishi*, is considered the founder of Buddhism in Japan. As the **regent** under Empress Suiko, he **issued an edict** promoting Buddhism and encouraging the building of temples. He is said to have ordered the construction of Shitennoji in 593 and, later, Horyuji. His connection with Horyuji is significant, because it became the center of admiration for his accomplishments.

In 604 Prince Shotoku issued a series of **precepts** based primarily on Buddhism, with the addition of Confucian **principles**. Together they are known as the Seventeen-Article Constitution. It was the first step in changing the political system from one based on **clans** to one based on imperial authority. A second step was the introduction of a new system of **court ranks**, known as "twelve cap ranks" (*kan'i junikai*). This granted status to individuals on the basis of merit, not **lineage**, and, importantly, status was not **hereditary**.

Buddhism was not universally welcomed. It was a new religion of foreign origin, and it was a threat to local **Shinto deities** and the powers of the traditional elite. After considerable conflict, a solution was reached. The emperor was to continue to serve as the high priest of the domestic *kami* worship and also be the chief **patron** of Buddhism.

Although Japan had **ambivalent** feelings toward China during the years after Prince Shotoku, Buddhism continued to adopt ideas, architectural styles, and poetry forms from China. It influenced writing, the legal system, philosophy, and art, through the medium of Buddhism. Prince Shotoku's first steps made it all possible. (254)

聖徳太子

日本の仏教の創始者

[574-622]

　聖徳太子は日本の仏教の創始者とされている。推古天皇の摂政として仏教を広めて寺院の建立を奨励し、593年に四天王寺、のちに法隆寺の建立を命じたといわれている。法隆寺とのつながりは、聖徳太子の功績を評価する上で中心をなしているため、とくに重要である。

　604年には、仏教を下敷きにした一連の規範に儒教の考え方を追加したいわゆる憲法十七条を制定した。これは、政治制度を氏姓制度から天皇の権威に基づく制度に移行する第1段階となるものだった。第2段階となるのが、冠位十二階の制として知られる新たな官位制度の導入だ。この官位は、家柄ではなく功績を基に個人に付与される身分で、重要なのは、この身分が世襲制ではないことだった。

　当時、仏教は万人に受け入れられておらず、他国から伝来した新興の宗教として、日本古来の神道や既存の特権階級が掌握していた権力への脅威となっていた。しかし、さまざまな対立を経て歩み寄りがなされ、天皇は引き続き神道の神を信仰する祭司としての役割を果たしながら、仏教の第一の庇護者という立場に就いた。

　聖徳太子の時代以降、しばらく日本は中国に相反する感情を抱いていたが、仏教においては中国の思想や建築様式、韻文を導入し続け、仏教を通じて、その影響は書や法制度、哲学、芸術に及んだ。それを可能にしたのは、聖徳太子が第一歩を踏み出したおかげだ。

■ regent 摂政　■ issue an edict 布告する　■ precept 教訓　■ principle 原理
■ clan 一族　■ court rank 官位　■ lineage 家柄　■ hereditary 世襲の
■ Shinto deity 神道　■ patron 後援者　■ ambivalent 相反する

03 Kakinomoto no Hitomaro

The First Esteemed Poet

Although we have little **concrete** knowledge of his career, Kakinomoto no Hitomaro **is regarded as** Japan's greatest poet of the ancient era. It is believed that he was a low-ranking member of the **courts** of Emperor Temmu, Empress Jito, and Emperor Mommu.

Emperor Tenmu, wishing to **incorporate** native elements **into** court rituals, invited people from the provinces who could compose poetry to the court. Hitomaro was already known for his poetry and he entered the service of the Empress, who later became Empress Jito.

Under her patronage, Hitomaro became an official court poet, whose job it was to **turn out** poems in praise or **commemoration** of the imperial family. They included **paeans**, **dirges**, and **ceremonial** poems. Some of these poems of formal events are like **overtures** to the imperial line and the land itself. But he also wrote works of a more personal character, many revealing a profound inner sorrow. Many poems **attributed to** him cannot be safely **verified**, but the ones that are clearly his are of such high quality that many people consider him the greatest Japanese poet.

Hitomaro is remembered as the most important poet of the *Man'yoshu*, the earliest anthology of Japanese verse. His style is both natural and complex. He masters pillow words (*makurakotoba*) and **irony** and **infuses** public events **with** personal emotions. He **universalizes** the intimate. Considered the best of the poets in this anthology, he ranks with Saigyo and Basho as one of the three most esteemed poets in Japanese culture. (248)

柿本人麻呂

日本文学の美的価値の礎

［生没年不詳］

　古代日本の最高の歌人とされる柿本人麻呂については具体的な経歴はほとんど分かっていないが、天武天皇、持統天皇、文武天皇に仕えた下級官吏だったとされる。

　日本古来の儀礼を宮廷に取り入れたいと考えた天武天皇は、地方から歌人を宮廷に招いた。人麻呂はすでに歌人として知られており、天武天皇の皇后である、のちの持統天皇に仕えた。

　持統天皇の庇護を受けて公式の宮廷歌人となった人麻呂は、天皇家をたたえ、故人をしのぶ歌を詠んだ。そうした歌には賛歌や挽歌、儀式の歌などがあり、公式行事に関する歌には皇統や日本国そのものを詠んだものもある。一方で、より私的な歌も詠んでおり、その多くには内面にかかえた深い悲哀が表れている。人麻呂が詠んだとされる歌の多くの真贋は定かではないが、間違いなく人麻呂が詠んだ歌は非常に優れており、多くの人に人麻呂は日本最高の歌人と見なされている。

　人麻呂は、（現存する）日本最古の歌集『万葉集』の最重要歌人として名を残している。そのスタイルは自然かつ複雑で、人麻呂は枕詞と反語法を駆使しながら、公的な行事に個人的な感情を織り込んだ歌を詠み、私的な関係を普遍化している。『万葉集』で最も優れた歌人と見なされた人麻呂は、西行（p.32）、松尾芭蕉（p.80）と並んで日本文化で最も尊敬されている詩人の一人に数えられている。

■ concrete 具体的な　　■ be regarded as 〜と見なされる　　■ court 宮廷
■ incorporate 〜 into … 〜を…に取り入れる　■ under one's patronage 〜の庇護を受けて　■ turn out 〜を作り出す　■ commemoration 追悼　■ paean 賛歌
■ dirge 葬送歌　■ ceremonial 儀式の　■ overture (詩・文の) 序章　■ attributed
to 〜の作であると考えられている　■ verify 真実性を証明する　■ irony 反語的表現
■ infuse 〜 with … 〜に…を注入する　■ universalize 一般化する

04 Gyoki
Buddhism for Ordinary People

When Buddhism was first introduced to Japan, it was **adopted** by the government to "protect the nation." The emperors and the **nobility** cultivated relations with elite Buddhist priests, and priests lived in government-sponsored temples. In short, there was almost no connection between Buddhism or Buddhist priests and the common people. The activities of an ordinary priest named Gyoki changed that.

Gyoki did not focus on the elite in the capital city of Nara, but instead traveled around the **countryside** preaching to ordinary people and **converting** them to Buddhism. Instead of building temples, he constructed places that might be called **chapels**, where people could gather and hear the **dharma**.

To improve the lives of ordinary people, he promoted projects such as the construction of bridges, **drainage canals**, and **aqueducts**. He did this by organizing the people he converted. Under heavy taxation and during epidemics and natural disasters, his teachings and leadership increased the productivity of ordinary farmers. In addition, he organized **charity houses** which, in times of famine, offered meals and lodging to the **destitute**.

Originally treated as an ordinary priest, he gradually became recognized for his leadership. His ability to organize people and gather contributions toward the construction of the Great Buddha (*Daibutsu*) of Todaiji in Nara was a special factor in changing the government's attitude toward him. Eventually, he became recognized as a high-ranking "master priest." We remember him not for **obtaining** high status but for his efforts at spreading Buddhism among the common people and his efforts toward improving their welfare during **perilous** times. (256)

行基

仏教の民間布教に尽力

[668-749]

　仏教が日本に伝来した当初、朝廷は国家を護持するために仏教を取り入れた。天皇や貴族は高僧との関係を深め、僧侶らは朝廷が後ろ盾となっている寺に住み、一般庶民は仏教とも僧侶ともほぼ無縁だった。そうした状況を変えたのが、一介の僧侶にすぎなかった行基の活動だった。

　行基は、都・奈良の特権階級を相手にする代わりに地方を行脚して庶民に説法を行い、仏教に改宗させ、寺ではなく、人々が集まって説法を聴ける道場を建てた。

　さらに庶民の暮らしを改善するため、橋や水路、堀などの建設を推進。こうした土木工事を、自身が改宗させた信者の集団を組織化して行った。農民たちは重い年貢や疫病、自然災害に苦しめられていたが、行基の教えと統率力で生産性を向上させていった。また、行基が造った救護施設である布施屋は、飢饉のときには貧民に食事と宿泊場所を提供する場となった。

　当初、行基は一僧侶扱いされていたが、次第に統率力を評価されるようになる。朝廷は行基に対する態度を改め、奈良の東大寺で大仏を造営する際の民衆に対する組織力と勧進力の高さから、やがて（仏教界最高位の）大僧正として認めるようになった。行基が今なお人々に記憶されているのは、高い地位に上り詰めたからではなく、民間に仏教を広め、苦難の時期に庶民の福祉の充実を図ったためだ。

■ adopt 取り入れる　■ nobility（the 〜で）上流階級　■ countryside 田舎　■ convert 〜を改宗させる　■ chapel 礼拝堂　■ dharma 仏陀の教え　■ drainage canal 排水路　■ aqueduct 水道橋　■ charity house 救護施設　■ destitute（the 〜で）困窮した人々　■ obtain 獲得する　■ perilous 危機に瀕した

05 Empress Komyo
Donator of Treasures to Shosoin

Komyo was not a reigning empress, but rather the **consort** (*kogo*) of Emperor Shomu. She was also the daughter of the powerful court official Fujiwara no Fuhito and the first woman not of royal blood to attain the rank of empress. She gave birth to a daughter who reigned as Empress Koken. During her daughter's reign, Komyo is believed to have **wielded** real **power** of government.

However, Komyo is remembered for two very different reasons. The first is that she generously sponsored two types of charitable foundations. **Refuges** for the poor and the **orphaned** (*hiden'in*) and **medical dispensaries** (*seyakuin*) for the sick may have been established by Prince Shotoku. But dependable records show that in 730 both types of institutions came under her sponsorship. She is credited with actively supporting them.

Secondly, she is also remembered for dedicating hundreds of valuable objects used by her husband Emperor Shomu and his court to the Great Buddha (*Daibutsu*) at Todaiji in Nara. More than six hundred of these are preserved today in the Shosoin, the **treasure house** of Todaiji. Her donations are one of two sources for the core collection of that storehouse.

The other source is articles that were transferred from a sub-temple of Todaiji. The articles include **calligraphy**, official documents, costumes, weapons, **ritual objects**, ceramics, and textiles. The majority of the treasures were made in Japan, but many reflect foreign sources in their motifs, materials, and methods of production. Tang China is the most direct influence, but some works in the collection reflect the cultures of India, Greece, and Persia. (260)

光明皇后

正倉院に宝物を寄進

［701-760］

　光明皇后は女帝ではなく、聖武天皇の皇后。朝廷の有力者、藤原不比等の娘で、皇族以外で初めて皇后となった。娘は孝謙天皇として即位するが、光明皇后は娘の治世に政務の実権を握っていたとみられている。

　光明皇后が後世に記憶されている理由は二つある。一つ目は、2種類の慈善団体を設立したことだ。貧しい人々や孤児のための救済施設（悲田院）と病に苦しむ人々のための診療所（施薬院）である。施薬院については聖徳太子が設立した可能性もあるが、730年に光明皇后の後押しで設立されたとする信憑性の高い記録が残っており、光明皇后はこうした施設を積極的に支援したと考えられている。

　二つ目は、光明皇后が夫の聖武天皇ゆかりの宝物と同天皇時代の朝廷が使用した貴重な品々を多数、奈良の東大寺の大仏に奉献したことだ。このうち600点以上は現在、東大寺の宝物庫、正倉院に保管されており、光明皇后の寄進した品々は正倉院の収蔵品の二大資財の一つを成している。

　正倉院のもう一つの重要な資財は、東大寺の堂宇から移された書や公文書、装束、武器、法具、陶器、織物などだ。宝物の大多数は日本で作られたものだが、文様や素材、制作方法などは異国風のものが多い。最も直接的な影響を受けているのは唐のものだが、インドやギリシャ、ペルシャなどの文化を反映した品物もある。

■consort（王・女王の）配偶者　■wield（影響力などを）振るう　■power 権力
■refuge 避難所　■orphaned（the 〜で）孤児　■medical dispensary 診療所
■treasure house 宝物庫　■calligraphy 書　■ritual object 法具

06 Emperor Kanmu
Founder of the Kyoto Capital

In the early period of Japanese history, the capital was moved several times, especially following the death of one emperor and the **ascendance** of a new emperor. When Emperor Kanmu, *Kanmu Tenno*, succeeded to the throne, he did two things that were particularly important in Japanese history.

One was to move the capital from Heijo-kyo (Nara) to Nagaoka-kyo (Kyoto)(in 784) and then to Heian-kyo (Kyoto)(in 794). It was a period when the centrally dominated ritsuryo system of **land allocation** and taxation was weakening, and Kanmu wanted to **distance** the seat of **secular** power **from** that of the major Buddhist temples, which were gathered in Nara. To prevent them from continuing to **interfering** in government affairs, he limited the construction of major temples in the new capital for a time.

However, Kanmu still needed the support of Buddhism for his government. Therefore, his second contribution was to become a generous patron of the **monks** Saicho and Kukai.

Learning of the reputation of Saicho on Mt. Hiei, Kanmu appointed Saicho as a priest serving the imperial court and in 804, he sent Saicho to China to gain formal training in T'ien-t'ai Buddhism. Kanmu also learned about Kukai's wealth of knowledge and lack of political ambition, and he sent Kukai to China as well.

The power and prestige of the imperial throne reached a peak during his **reign**. (226)

桓武天皇

京都に日本の都を移す

［737-806］

　日本の歴史の初期にはたびたび遷都が行われ、特に天皇が崩御し、次の天皇が即位するタイミングで都が移されることが多かった。桓武天皇は、自身が即位すると、日本史において特に重要な二つのことを実践した。

　一つ目は、都を784年に平城京（現・奈良）から長岡京（現・京都）に移し、さらに794年に平安京（現・京都）に遷都したことだ。土地の配分や年貢を定めた中央集権的な律令制が弱体化していたこの時期、桓武天皇は奈良に集中していた仏教の主要寺院（南都六宗）の勢力から世俗的な権力の座を遠ざけたいと考え、政務に口出しする寺院を切り離そうと、新都での主要寺院の建立をしばらく制限した。

　だが、仏教の支援なしでは、やはり朝廷は立ちゆかない。そこで桓武天皇の二つ目の功績となるのが、2人の僧、最澄（p.22）と空海（p.24）を手厚く庇護することだった。

　比叡山での最澄の評判を知った桓武天皇は、最澄を宮中に仕える僧官に任命し、804年には中国の唐に派遣して正式に天台宗を修学させた。また、空海が博覧強記で政治的野心もないことを知り、同じく唐に派遣したとされる。

　天皇の権力と威信は、桓武天皇の治世に絶頂を極めた。

■ascendance 即位　■land allocation 土地の配分　■distance ～ from … …から～を遠ざける　■secular 世俗的な　■interfere 干渉する　■monk 僧　■intrusion 侵入　■relocate 移転する　■reign 治世

07 Saicho
The Center of Buddhist Studies

Saicho became a priest at Todaiji but **became dissatisfied with** the priests who were concerned only about their own benefits and ceremonies for the government. Feeling the **transience** of **worldly things**, he left Nara, and in 785 built a hut on Mt. Hiei, northeast of Kyoto. It was a simple, harsh environment for religious practice. There he studied, practiced, and learned how to spread the true teachings of Buddhism.

When Emperor Kanmu moved the capital to Kyoto in 794, he heard about this **devout** priest. He sent Saicho to China to study Buddhism with the masters there.

Saicho collected Buddhist texts and received instruction on **T'ien-t'ai teachings**. When Saicho returned to Japan, he began **lecturing on** the Lotus Sutra and eventually established on Mt. Hiei a major center for Tendai Buddhism, an **offshoot** of the Chinese T'ien-t'ai sect. It became the **unparalleled** center of Buddhist studies in the country.

The Nara schools of Buddhism held that only certain people were capable of **attaining enlightenment**. In contrast to this elitist view, Saicho taught that all **sentient beings** are capable of enlightenment, a fundamental aspect of Mahayana Buddhism. Saicho taught that Tendai priests should devote their energies to saving others as a way of saving themselves. This became a highly influential belief in all forms of Japanese Buddhism.

Saicho is also remembered for stressing that religious organizations needed **autonomy**. He insisted that the government should not determine who could **be ordained** as a priest. Under his leadership, the national system of control over the priesthood came to an end. (257)

最澄

仏教学の礎を確立

[767-822]

　最澄は、東大寺の僧侶となるが、自分の利益や朝廷の儀式のことしか頭にない僧たちに**不満を抱き**、**諸行無常**を感じて奈良を離れ、785年に京都北東部の比叡山に草庵を建てた。宗教的な修行をするには、簡素で過酷な環境だった。ここで最澄は学んで修行し、仏教の真の教えを広める方法を会得した。

　桓武天皇（p.20）は、794年に京都に遷都した際に、この**敬虔**な僧、最澄の話を聞き知り、その後、高僧から仏教を学ばせるために最澄を唐に派遣した。

　最澄は経典を集め、**天台教学**の教義を学ぶ。帰国すると、法華経の教えを説き始め、ついには、比叡山に中国を発祥とする天台教学の宗派、天台宗の一大拠点を設け、この地は、国内で並ぶもののない仏教学の中心となった。

　奈良仏教（南都六宗）は、特権階級のみが悟りを開けるという考えを基にしていた。こうした特権階級的な考えとは対照的に、最澄は、**一切衆生**が悟りを開くことができるという大乗仏教の基本的な考え方を教え、天台宗の僧は、己を救うように他者を救うことに力を注ぐべきという**忘己利他**の教えを説いた。この考えは、日本の仏教のあらゆる宗派に非常に大きな影響を及ぼしていく。

　最澄は、宗教団体の**自律性**を訴えたことでも知られ、朝廷が出家や授戒を認める権限を持つべきではないと主張した。最澄の主導により、国家が僧職を管理する体制は終わりを迎えた。

■became dissatisfied with 〜に不満を抱く　■transience はかなさ　■worldly things 世俗的なもの　■devout 信心深い　■T'ien-t'ai teachings 天台教学　■lecture on 〜について説く　■offshoot 支流　■unparalleled 無比の　■attain enlightenment 悟りを得る　■sentient beings 一切衆生　■autonomy 自治権　■be ordained 任命される

08 Kukai

Transmitter of Esoteric Buddhism

Kukai left Shikoku to study Confucian, Taoist, and Buddhist teachings in Kyoto. He mastered the Chinese classics, but gave up a future career as an official to become a mountain **ascetic**, visiting **secluded** holy places on Shikoku.

Given the rare chance to study in Tang China, he studied **Esoteric Buddhism** with the master Keika (Huiguo). Showing exceptional talent, Kukai was instructed in the ultimate secret teachings and he received formal **transmission** of the major esoteric teachings. Subsequently, Kukai became the eighth patriarch of Chen-yen (Esoteric) Buddhism.

This direct line of transmission crossed to Japan when Kukai returned with **sutras**, images, and **ritual implements** essential for carrying out Buddhist ceremonies. He founded Shingon Buddhism and won the support of the emperor, establishing a **monastery** on Mt. Koya called Kongobuji in 816. In addition, he **was entrusted with** Toji Temple in Kyoto.

Upon his death, he was given the **posthumous title** Kobo Daishi, "great teacher who spread teachings." In addition to his **documented accomplishments**, oral traditions and folklore attribute other achievements to him. He **is credited with** building dams and irrigation ponds, discovering springs, and sculpting images of Buddha.

These legends show a special relationship that developed between Kukai and common people. Many of the miracles resulted from his charisma and the confidence people had in him. When he called local people to work together, they were able to **accomplish legendary feats**. People honor him today by taking part in the Shikoku pilgrimage of 88 temples, (*Shikoku henro*). (252)

空海

日本の密教の祖

[774-835]

　空海は四国（現・香川）から京に上り、儒教、道教、仏教を学んだ。漢学も習得したが、役人になる道を捨てて山で修験者となり、四国の人里離れた霊場を訪れた。

　得難い機会に恵まれて唐に留学。恵果和尚の下で密教を学び、ずば抜けて優秀であったため究極の秘法を教わり、密教の奥義を正式に伝授された。のちに、空海は真言八祖（真言宗で崇拝される8人の祖師）の第八祖となった。

　直伝の密教奥義が日本に伝わったのは、空海が帰国したときだ。このとき空海は、仏事を行う際に欠かせない経典や仏画、法具なども日本に伝えた。その後、真言宗を開き、816年に天皇に賜った高野山に僧院、金剛峰寺を建立。また、京の東寺（教王護国寺）も下賜された。

　仏教の教えを広く伝えた「弘法利生」の業績により、諡号は「弘法大師」。空海の功績は書物に記されているだけでなく、空海によるものとされる口承や伝承がいくつもあり、堰や灌漑池を建設した、泉を発見した、仏像を彫ったなどの話が残っている。

　こうした伝説は、空海と市井の人々が特別な関係を築いていた表れでもある。奇跡の伝説の多くは、空海のカリスマ性と人々の信頼から生まれたものだ。空海は地元の人々に協力を呼び掛け、ともに偉業を達成した。今日も人々は四国八十八カ所を巡礼（四国遍路）して空海を敬っている。

■ ascetic 修行者　■ secluded 人里離れた　■ Esoteric Buddhism 密教
■ transmission 伝授　■ sutra 経典　■ ritual implement 法具　■ monastery
（主に男子の）修道院　■ be entrusted with 〜を受託される　■ posthumous
title 死後の称号　■ documented 文書化された　■ accomplishment 功績　■ be
credited with 〜の功績があると信じられている　■ accomplish 達成する
■ legendary feat 伝説的な功績

09 Ono no Komachi
Dramatic Palace Poet

Ono no Komachi is one of the great *waka* poets of the Heian period. She is one of the *Rokkasen*, the Six Poetic Geniuses, according to Ki no Tsurayuki, **compiler** of the *Kokinshu*. And she became an example of the classical elite.

It is hard to separate the historical woman from the legends that formed around her. The latter treat her as a woman of passion, a beauty, and a lover. She has **fed the imaginations** of many poets and lovers of literature. Thought to have been a **palace attendant**, her poems tend to be about either unhappy or **unrequited** love, separation, or being betrayed by lovers. Those in the *Kokinshu* are remarkably intense and they stand out among the others. In this sense, she started a tradition that continues to Yosano Akiko in the present era.

She is not the only poet to use *kakekotoba*, a "pivot word," in which a series of sounds can mean two things. For example, in a poem the word *akashi* can mean the name of a place, Akashi, or the verb "dawn". In a short poem, this technique **conveys** dual possibilities, and Ono no Komachi uses this both frequently and very effectively.

The stories about Komachi became basic to later understanding of the Heian court and the ideals it represented. As a result, she became the subject of a number of literary works. The great masters of Noh drama, Kan'ami and Zeami, **took** her **up** in five plays in the 14th and 15th centuries. Mishima Yukio took her up in his modern Noh play *Sotoba Komachi*. (263)

小野小町

ドラマチックな宮廷歌人

［生没年不詳］

　小野小町は、平安時代の優れた歌人の一人だ。『古今和歌集』の撰者の一人、紀貫之に六歌仙（6人の代表的な歌人）の一人に挙げられ、和歌の代表的歌人となった。

　歴史上の人物であるが、小町をその伝説と切り離すのは難しい。後世の人々に情熱的な女性、絶世の美女、恋多き女性として伝えられ、多くの詩人や文学愛好家の想像をかき立ててきた。宮仕えしていたとされる小町の歌は、切ない恋や片思い、別れ、恋人からの裏切りをテーマにしたものが多く、『古今和歌集』に収められている歌は非常に鮮烈で、他の歌より際立っている。小町から始まるそうした伝統は、近代の与謝野晶子（p.144）に受け継がれている。

　小町は他の歌人と同じく、ある言葉に二つの意味を持たせる掛詞を用いている。例えば、和歌に出てくる「あかし」という掛詞は、場合によって地名の「明石」を指すと同時に「夜が明ける」という動詞を意味する。この修辞技法は短い歌の中で二重の意味を伝え、小町はこの技法をたびたび、そして非常に効果的に使っている。

　小町に関するさまざまな話は、のちに、平安時代の宮中と、宮中で理想とされた概念を理解する基礎となった。そうして小町は数々の文学作品のテーマとなり、能楽の大家、観阿弥と世阿弥（p.52）は14世紀から15世紀にかけて5本の謡曲に小野小町を登場させ、三島由紀夫（p.208）は近代能楽の戯曲『卒塔婆小町』（観阿弥の翻案作品）で取り上げている。

■compiler 編纂者　■feed the imaginations 想像をかき立てる　■palace attendant 女官　■unrequited love 報われない恋　■convey 伝える　■take ～ up ～を取り上げる

10 Murasaki Shikibu
The World's First Novel

The *Tale of Genji* (*Genji monogatari*) is the supreme masterpiece in the history of Japanese prose literature and is considered the first novel in world literature. It is the story of "the shining Prince Genji," his life and loves, followed by the less **auspicious** life of Kaoru.

Very little is known about Murasaki Shikibu's life. The **sobriquet** by which she is commonly known may refer to the Fujiwara family or to the *Shiki-busho*, Ministry of Rites, where her father was once an official. The name Murasaki, "purple," may refer to the wisteria of her family name or refer to the great love of Genji's life.

It is believed that she spent her early years in the imperial capital of Heian-kyo, married, had one daughter, and **was widowed** in 1001. She **was summoned to** the imperial court as a **lady-in-waiting** to the Empress Shoshi. She probably began writing the *Tale of Genji* in the early years of her widowhood, and because of its appeal she was called to the imperial court.

Murasaki Shikibu was the greatest innovator in the art of prose fiction, certainly in Japan and perhaps in the world. Her imagination was essentially dramatic, making its points and conveying meanings through the portrayal of her characters. She portrays the **complexities** of the human spirit and a believable individual life on the written page. She does this through strong, credible characters rather than through **simile** and **metaphor**, the literary devices of traditional Japanese literature.

The *Tale of Genji* has had an enormous influence on later Japanese literature and other arts forms, and has been adapted for Kabuki, cinema, and television. (270)

紫式部

世界初の小説を執筆

［生没年不詳］

　紫式部による『源氏物語』は、日本の散文作品史上最高傑作で、世界初の小説とされ、貴族光源氏の恋多き生涯と、薫大将の幸薄い人生を描いている。

　紫式部がどのような生涯をたどったかは分かっていないことが多い。一般的に知られている紫式部という呼称は、（父方の）藤原家から来ているという説もあれば、父のかつての官位、式部省に由来するという説もある。紫という名は、姓の藤の色にちなんでいるとも、光源氏が生涯で最も愛した「紫の上」にちなんでいるともいわれている。

　幼い頃は平安京で過ごし、結婚して娘を一人もうけ、1001年に夫と死別したとみられている。彰子皇后の女房として宮廷に召し出されるが、夫に先立たれて間もなくしてから『源氏物語』を書き始め、その評判から宮廷に呼ばれたのではないかとされている。

　散文小説の技術に関しては、日本では間違いなく、そしておそらく世界でも最大の革新者と言って過言ではない。式部の創作力は基本的にドラマチックなもので、登場人物の描写を通じて意図を伝え、心の機微や、血の通った人物の人生をつづっている。式部はそうした表現を、日本文学の伝統的技法である直喩や暗喩ではなく、パワフルで説得力のある登場人物の描写によってものにしている。

　『源氏物語』は、後世の日本文学やその他さまざまな芸術作品に非常に大きな影響を与え、歌舞伎や映画、テレビでも翻案されている。

■auspicious 幸運な　■sobriquet あだ名　■be widowed 配偶者に先立たれる　■be summoned to ～に召喚される　■lady-in-waiting 侍女　■complexity 複雑さ　■simile 直喩　■metaphor 暗喩

11 Sei Shonagon
Brilliant Social Observor

Author of "The Pillow Book of Sei Shonagon" (*Makura no soshi*), Sei Shonagon is one of the best known of the brilliant writers of the Heian period. This short work belongs in the genre known as *zuihitsu*, meaning "to follow the brush." This uniquely Japanese genre term describes a free-flowing perspective on life as it unfolds. The Pillow Book is composed of rather casual essays, spur-of-the-moment impressions, reflections on daily events, and imagined scenes. It is a **discursive lyrical** essay, a form that the Japanese have **been** very **fond of** over the centuries.

Sei Shonagon is the name she is known by, based on her position in the imperial court. She became a lady-in-waiting at the court of the Empress Teishi, the **consort** of the young Emperor Ichijo. She began composing her "pillow book" after her debut at court and continued it through her years of service. Little is known about what happened to her after Teishi died, but tradition has it that she ended her days old and impoverished.

Makura no soshi is a literary **masterpiece**, but also a work of historical significance because it details the events and customs of the Heian court. More importantly, it provides a clear view of the author's personality and style. She delights in the moment and does not **dwell on** it after it passes. She is **opinionated** and **abrasive** at times, but she has a rare sensitivity to the events and her impressions are **poignant**. While she did not attempt a full-blown novel like her contemporary Murasaki Shikibu, her precise, **evocative** observations seem modern and entertaining even today. (266)

清少納言

鋭敏なる社会観察者

［生没年不詳］

　『枕草子』の著者、清少納言は、平安時代の優れた作家の中でも最も有名な一人。短編をまとめた『枕草子』は、「筆に従う」ことを意味する「随筆」というジャンルに属している。日本独自のこのジャンルは、人生観を自由気ままにつづったもので、『枕草子』は、何げないエッセーや、ふとした瞬間に感じたこと、日々の出来事の覚え書き、空想場面などで構成されている。とりとめのない、叙情的なエッセーは、何世紀にもわたって日本人に非常に好まれてきた形式だ。

　清少納言は、宮廷での地位に基づく名前とされている。清少納言は、若い一条天皇の皇后となった（藤原）定子の女房になり、宮仕えをするかたわら、『枕草子』を書き始めた。定子が亡くなった後、清少納言がどのような人生を送ったのかはほとんど分かっていないが、年老いてから困窮して亡くなったとの説もある。

　『枕草子』は文学の傑作であると同時に、平安時代の宮中の出来事や慣習を詳細につづっていることから、歴史的な意義を持つ作品でもある。さらに重要なのは、清少納言の人となりや、個人的な流儀がよく分かることだ。清少納言は、その瞬間を楽しみ、過去にはこだわらない。時に独断的で辛辣だが、さまざまな出来事に稀有な感性を持ち、捉え方が的を射ている。同時代の紫式部（p.28）のように本格的な小説を書こうとはしなかったが、的確で、**想像力を刺激する**観察は現代に通じ、今読んでも面白い。

■ discursive とりとめのない　■ lyrical 叙情的な　■ be fond of 〜が大好きである
■ consort 王・女王の配偶者　■ masterpiece 傑作　■ dwell on 〜についてあれこれ考える　■ opinionated 自己主張する　■ abrasive 人をいらだたせる
■ poignant 確信をついた　■ evocative 想像力を刺激する

12 Saigyo
Reclusive Poet Monk

The poet-monk Saigyo is famous for the **semireclusive** life he lived. It combined a deep love of beauty and a Buddhist sensitivity to the world. Leaving the capital of Kyoto, he **took residence on** remote Mt. Koya, a monastery of Shingon Buddhism. From there he began a series of walking tours to distant pilgrimage centers. Among the first of the great traveling poets, he composed poems (*waka*) about his solitary existence and his **aesthetic** responses to nature.

As a priest, he moved freely and met people of all social classes. As he grew older he developed relations with powerful nobles, military leaders, the great poet Fujiwara no Shunzei and **the latter's** famous son Fujiwara no Teika. In the final decade of his life, Shinto priests of the Ise Shrine and others came to him for instruction in composing poetry.

The collection of poems titled "The Mountain Hermitage" (*Sankashu*) contains some 1,600 of the 2,000 poems attributed to him. His poems are included in several imperial anthologies, and in the great *Shin Kokinshu* (compiled in about 1205), one finds 94 poems by Saigyo, more than any other poet. His poetry embraces *sabi*, a sense of lonely, **austere beauty**, with a spirit of **lyric melancholy**.

Saigyo is perhaps **comparable** only **to** the great haikai poet Basho, who he profoundly influenced. His poems are deeply **evocative**, yet feel breathtakingly simple. His best poems are unmatched, and were appreciated in his own day, as well as by later generations. (245)

西行

漂泊の法師歌人

[1118-1190]

　歌人であり、僧侶で（元武士で）もあった西行は、半ば隠遁生活を送ったことで知られる。その暮らしには、美に対する深い愛と世界に対する仏教的な視点が備わっていた。西行は京の都を離れたのち、人里離れた高野山に真言宗の草庵を構え、そこから遠方の巡礼地まで何度か遍路の旅に出た。漂泊の歌人の先駆けとして、自身の独居生活と自然に対する美的な感受性を和歌に詠んだ。

　西行は僧として自由に移動し、あらゆる社会階級の人々と出会い、年を重ねるにつれ、権力を持つ貴族や武将、優れた歌人の藤原俊成とその有名な息子、藤原定家（p.44）らとの関係を深めた。晩年には、自身の元を訪れる伊勢神宮の神官らに和歌を指導している。

　歌集『山家集』には、西行が詠んだとされる約2,000首のうち約1,600首が収められている。西行の和歌はいくつかの勅撰集にも収められているが、『新古今和歌集』（1205年頃に編纂）には、西行の和歌は歌人の中で最多となる94首が選ばれている。西行の和歌には、閑寂枯淡の美と叙情的な哀愁の精神を示す寂の概念が取り入れられている。

　偉大な俳人・松尾芭蕉（p.80）に肩を並べるのは西行だと言っても過言ではないかもしれない。芭蕉は西行から多大な影響を受けている。西行の歌は、さまざまな感情を深く揺さぶる一方で、驚くほどシンプルな印象がある。珠玉の歌の数々は無比の出来で、同時代だけでなく、後世の人々にも評価されている。

■ semireclusive 半ば隠遁した　　■ take residence on ～に居を構える
■ aesthetic 審美的な　■ the latter 後者　■ austere beauty 簡素な美　■ lyric
melancholy 叙情的な哀愁　■ comparable to ～に匹敵する　■ evocative 喚起する

13 Honen
Making Buddhism Accessible

As a young man, Honen went to Mt. Hiei to study T'ien-t'ai Buddhism, but he grew **discontented**. Honen had believed that he could **attain enlightenment** through his own powers, but he was unsuccessful. Then he found a Buddhist commentary which taught that **ordinary beings** do not have the ability to gain enlightenment on their own. He realized that the best way was to rely completely on the accumulated merit and power of Amida Buddha. All one had to do was to **invoke** Amida's name. This offered people a new religious hope for salvation called "other power" (*tariki*), contrasting with "own power" (self-power, *jiriki*) that other **sects** aimed for. It was a watershed in the history of Japanese Buddhism.

Honen departed Mt. Hiei and began teaching "the exclusive practice of the *nenbutsu*," invoking the name of the Amida Buddha. He gave up the idea that one had to become a priest to gain **salvation**. The message he preached challenged the older Nara schools, the Mt. Hiei priests, and the government.

Honen founded the Jodo sect of Pure Land Buddhism, which is known for preaching the *nembutsu*, the phrase "*Namu Amida Butsu*" or "I believe in the Amida Buddha." This required no priests, no temples, and no complex practices. Just saying this phrase enough times before death allows a believer to be reborn in the Pure Land. As a result, he was **banished** because others saw his **insistence** on this "exclusive practice" as a threat, denying practices such as **meditation** and teachings. However, his teachings greatly appealed to ordinary people and he drew a large following. (264)

法然

他力本願を唱えて仏教を普及

［1133-1212］

　若い頃の法然は、比叡山で天台宗を学んでいたが、次第に不満を募らせていった。己の力で悟りを開くことができると考えていたが、それがかなわず、凡夫は自分で悟りを得られないとする仏教の経典を見つけ、阿弥陀如来の功徳と力にひたすら頼ることが最善の道だと悟る。阿弥陀仏の名を唱えるだけでいいとするこの考えは、他の宗派が目指していた「自力」とは対照的に「他力」と呼ばれ、自分も救済を得られるという新たな宗教的な希望を人々に与え、日本の仏教史上の分岐点となった。

　法然は比叡山を離れ、阿弥陀仏の名を唱える「専修念仏」の教えを説き始め、僧にならなければ救われないという考えを捨てた。法然が提唱した考えは、奈良の従来の宗派や比叡山の僧侶、朝廷と真っ向から対立した。

　このころ法然は浄土宗を開宗する。これは、「私は阿弥陀仏に帰依します」を意味する「南無阿弥陀仏」という念仏を説くことで知られる宗派で、僧侶も寺も複雑な修行も必要とせず、生前にこの念仏をひたすら唱えるだけで極楽浄土に生まれ変われるというものである。その結果、瞑想や仏法を否定するこの「唯一の教え」は脅威と見なされ、法然は流罪となる。だが、その教えは庶民の心をつかみ、多くの信徒を集めた。

■ discontented 不満な　■ attain enlightenment 悟りを開く　■ ordinary being 普通の人　■ invoke（神）の名を呼ぶ　■ sect 宗派　■ salvation 救済　■ banish 流刑に処す　■ insistence 主張　■ meditation 瞑想

14 Unkei
Sculptor of Dynamism

The Kei school (*kei-ha*) of **sculptors** of Buddhist images who were active mostly during the Kamakura period took kei as part of their names. Unkei was the son of Kokei, a **contemporary of** Kaikei, and the father of Tankei.

Unkei is considered the greatest master of the Kei school. He gradually abandoned the Nara period preference for idealized, **formulaic**, delicate forms. He **revitalized** the art of sculpture with figures which were unlike any others. They were lifelike, muscular, realistic forms, in dramatic poses. It **is speculated** that he even used well-built sumo wrestlers as models.

Although based in Nara and Kyoto, he also accepted **commissions** from samurai and high-ranking officials in Kamakura, base of the warrior-based shogunate. Not surprisingly, his realistic style and **depictions** of muscular male bodies appealed to the warriors of the period.

Unfortunately, many of Unkei's work have been lost. The Kofukuji Temple and Todaiji Temples in Nara have many of his **extant** works. Elsewhere, works that can **be attributed to** him with certainty include one of Dainichi Nyorai (Mahavairocana) at Ennjoji in Nara, an Amida Triad, a Fudo Myoo, and a Bishamonten.

In 1203, he worked with Kaikei and other master sculptors to create the two guardian deity statues known as *Nio* (Benevolent Kings), for the Great South Gate, *Nandaimon*, of Todaiji in Nara. These figures were 26 feet tall and **were sculpted from** various pieces of wood that were then assembled together. Among his less imposing works, *rakan* figures of Mujaku and Seshin of Kofukuji Temple are so natural that they seem like specific people rather than **stock characters**. (264)

運慶

ダイナミズムの仏師

［?-1223］

　主に鎌倉時代に活躍した仏師の一派、慶派は、名前に慶の1字を付けた仏師を多く輩出した。運慶は康慶の子で、湛慶の父。快慶と同時代に活躍した。

　運慶は慶派で最も優れた仏師とされている。奈良時代に好まれ、理想化されていた、月並みで繊細な造形から徐々に脱却し、ほかに類を見ない作風で彫刻芸術に新しい命を吹き込んだ。運慶の作品は、ドラマチックなポーズで、まるで生きているかのように筋骨隆々で、写実的な造形をしている。体格の良い力士をモデルにしていたともいわれている。

　運慶は奈良と京都を拠点にしていたが、幕府のお膝元、鎌倉の武士や御家人からの依頼にも応じていた。写実的な作風と筋骨隆々とした男性の肉体の描写は、当然のことながら、当時の武士に人気があった。

　残念ながら、運慶の作品の多くは失われてしまったが、奈良の興福寺や東大寺には、いくつもの作品が残されている。ほかにも、奈良・円成寺の大日如来坐像や、（神奈川・浄楽寺の）阿弥陀三尊像、不動明王立像、毘沙門天立像などは間違いなく運慶作とされる。

　1203年には、快慶ら優れた仏師と協力して、奈良・東大寺南大門に設置する2体の守護神像、仁王（金剛力士）像を制作。像の高さは約8メートルで、多数の木材から成る寄木造の技法で彫刻されている。興福寺の、もう少し小ぢんまりとした羅漢像（無著・世親立像）は非常に自然で、類型的な架空の人物ではなく、実在の人物らしい特徴をよく捉えている。

■ sculptor 彫刻家　■ contemporary of 〜と同時代の人　■ formulaic 月並みな
■ revitalize 活性化する　　■ be speculated 推測される　　■ commission 注文
■ depiction 描写　■ extant 残存する　■ be attributed to 〜の作品とされる
■ be sculpted from 〜から彫刻される　■ stock character（フィクションの）お決まりの人物

15 Kamo no Chomei

Aesthetic Recluse

A **courtier** turned religious **recluse**, Kamo no Chomei wrote an important literary account of a pivotal age in Japanese history. "An Account of My **Hut**" (*Hojoki*) describes the **insubstantiality** of life and a world that is always in **flux**. Yet it makes no mention of the struggle between the Taira and Minamoto in the early 1180s. Instead, it describes a series of natural disasters, including fires, famine, and earthquakes. Chomei presents in Buddhist terms a pessimistic view of life.

To escape it, Chomei renounces all **worldly attachments** and prepares himself for Amida's Pure Land paradise upon death. However, he fails to gain release from **earthly concerns**. In fact, he has become attached even to his simple, remote hut.

Chomei's work is a superb description of an **aesthetic** that developed during the medieval period: a preference for simplicity, restraint, weathered **austerity** (*wabi, sabi*). This ideal reaches a peak several centuries later in the tea ceremony. Under the influence of Zen Buddhism, tea masters built teahouses on the model of a **peasant** hut. Although the teahouse may be in a city, it will be designed as though it is in natural surroundings in some remote mountain. The tea master will assume the role of someone who had **withdrawn from the world** and seeks **tranquility** in the enjoyment of tea.

"An Account of My Hut" is a landmark in Japanese literary and philosophical consciousness. The **refined** tranquillity of the hut described in this work makes the translations of this work very appealing to foreigners who study Japan. (254)

鴨長明

優れた審美眼の隠遁者

[1155?-1216]

　宮廷に仕えながら、その後、出家し、隠遁生活を送った鴨長明は、意義のある文学的な記録を残し、日本史の重要な時代（鎌倉時代）を伝えている。その書、『方丈記』では、無常観と有為転変を描いている。1180年代初頭の平家と源氏の争いについては一切触れず、火事、飢饉、地震など、さまざまな自然災害を取り上げ、仏教的な無常観を提示している。

　長明は俗世から逃れ、この世へのこだわりを一切捨て、阿弥陀如来の極楽浄土に向かう準備をするが、俗世の煩悩からは解放されず、それどころか、人里離れた自身の草庵に愛着を抱くようになっていった。

　長明の作品には、中世に成熟した、簡素で抑制の利いた侘び寂を好む美学が見事に表現されている。この美意識が花開くのは、それから数百年後、茶道においてである。茶人らは、禅宗の影響を受け、草庵を模範として茶室を建てた。茶室は、そこが都市だとしても、人里離れた山の中で自然に囲まれているかのように設計され、茶人は、俗世間を離れた隠遁者の役割を担い、茶を味わうことに静寂を求める。

　『方丈記』は日本文学と哲学的な意識における金字塔である。この中に描かれている草庵の研ぎ澄まされた静けさは、日本を研究する外国人にとって、この作品をぜひとも翻訳してみたいと思わせる魅力に満ちている。

■courtier 宮廷に仕える人　■recluse 隠遁者　■hut 小屋　■insubstantiality 空虚さ　■flux 移り変わり　■worldly attachment 世俗的な愛慕　■earthly concern 俗世の煩悩　■aesthetic 美的価値　■austerity 簡素さ　■peasant 農民　■withdraw from the world 世間から引きこもる　■tranquility 静寂　■refined 洗練された

16 Hojo Masako
Power without a Title

Wife of the founder of the Kamakura shogunate, mother of the second and third shoguns, and daughter of the first regent, Hojo Masako sat at **the seat of power**. She became **arguably** the most powerful woman in **male-dominated** pre-modern Japan.

Her husband, Minamoto no Yoritomo, established himself at Kamakura as the court-appointed *Sei-i Taishogun*, "barbarian-subduing generalissimo." He controlled the majority of the Kanto Plain and was charged with maintaining the peace of the entire country. While his headquarters were known by the **humble** name *bakufu*, "tent government," he was the country's most powerful figure. However, Yoritomo died before achieving his ambition and he had no surviving children to succeed him. The family of his wife Hojo Masako began to **exert** influence as a variety of regent (*shikken*) for the shogun. In effect, the Hojo clan influenced not only the selection of the shogun, but also took control of administration in the capital, acting **on behalf of** the Kamakura shogunate.

Following Yoritomo's death, Masako took Buddhist vows, but she became involved in shogunate politics. As the "nun shogun" (*ama shogun*), she remained powerful in shogunate councils until her death. **Strong willed** and **single-minded**, she played a leading role in every event **crucial to** the establishment of the Kamakura shogunate. Though she never led warriors into battle and never took the title of shogun, she deserves to be called the "founder" of the Kamakura shogunate. (233)

北条政子

官位を持たない権力者

[1157-1225]

　北条政子は、鎌倉幕府を開いた源頼朝の妻で、2代将軍・頼家、3代将軍・実朝の母で、鎌倉幕府の初代執権である北条時政を父に持つ。（頼朝の死後に）幕政の実権を握り、**男性優位の近代以前の日本で最も権力のある女性**と言っても**過言**ではない。

　頼朝は、鎌倉で征夷大将軍に任官し、関東平野の大部分を支配下に収めて関東を平定する役割を担った。幕府には「陣中で幕を張った中で実務を行う政府」という**控えめな意味**があるが、頼朝は国内で最も武力を持つ人物だった。しかし頼朝は志半ばで急死し、後継となる子どもも断絶。妻である政子の一族が、執権として、将軍の代わりに影響力を振るうようになっていく。北条氏は、将軍として誰を立てるかという問題に影響を与えただけでなく、鎌倉幕府の**代表として都の施政**も行った。

　頼朝の死後、政子は出家するが、幕政に関わるようになり、「尼将軍」として、亡くなるまで幕府の評議で発言権を持った。**意志が強く、ひたむき**で、鎌倉幕府の成立に**欠かせない**あらゆる出来事で主導的な役割を果たした。武士を率いて出陣することも将軍の称号を得ることもなかったが、政子こそが鎌倉幕府の礎であったといえる。

■the seat of power 権力の座　■arguably ほぼ間違いなく　■male-dominated 男性優位の　■humble 謙遜した　■exert 行使する　■on behalf of ～に代わって　■strong willed 意志の強い　■single-minded ひたむきな　■crucial to ～に不可欠な

17 Minamoto no Yoshitsune
Popular Tragic Hero

Considered to be a great military commander and a tragic hero, Minamoto no Yoshitsune restored the honor of the Genji **clan** through a series of well-planned battles ending in the great **naval** victory at Dannoura in 1185. As a result, Yoshitsune made a major contribution to establishing a new form of government, **headed by** his brother Yoritomo. Yoshitsune had, in effect, supported his brother's **ascendance to** power. One would anticipate that Yoritomo would be grateful.

Whether it was because they were half-brothers who had been raised apart from one another, because they had different personalities, or because it was natural to be suspicious of a potential **competitor**, the relationship between Yoritomo and Yoshitsune grew tense. Fearing for his life, Yoshitsune fled north to **take refuge with** the Fujiwara in Hiraizumi, in northeast Japan.

Under orders from Yoritomo, troops pursued Yoshitsune and in 1189 he was forced to commit suicide. In addition, the political headquarters of the Fujiwara was also destroyed.

Yoshitsune's military exploits, his encounter with the powerful monk Benkei, and the mystery surrounding his **upbringing** have made him the subject of narratives, paintings, and theatrical performances. Yoshitsune lives in the popular imagination as an ideal Japanese hero who appeals to the national sensibility. He is daring, trusting, and **sincere**, but most of all he is loved for his **misfortune** and his ultimate defeat. His brilliant success was a requirement for his greatness, because it made his subsequent collapse even more impressive and **poignant**. His tragic defeat drew people's emotional identification with the loser. (254)

源義経

大衆に愛された悲劇の英雄

［1159-1189］

　名将で、悲劇の英雄といわれている 源 義経 は、巧みな戦術による戦い
を続け、源氏の名誉を回復し、1185年の海戦、壇の浦の戦いで（平家に）
大勝利する。それによって平家を滅ぼし、兄の 源 頼朝 が率いる新たな形
式の武家政権の確立に大きく貢献。兄が権力の座へと上り詰めていく実質
的な支えとなった。頼朝も、さぞ感謝したはずと思われた。

　だが、異母兄弟で別々に育ったせいか、性格の違いか、あるいは、いず
れ自分の敵になるのではないかと疑うのは自然な成り行きだったのか、頼
朝と義経は対立を強めていく。身の危険を感じた義経は、北上して東北地
方の平泉（岩手）の奥州藤原氏の下に逃れた。

　頼朝の命を受けた軍に追われた義経は1189年に自害を余儀なくされた。
また、奥州藤原氏の政庁も破壊された。

　義経の武勇伝や、怪力の僧兵・弁慶との出会い、謎の多い生い立ちは、
さまざまな物語や絵画、芝居のテーマとなってきた。義経は、日本人が理
想とするヒーローとして日本人の感性に訴え掛け、大衆のイマジネーショ
ンの中で息づいている。義経は大胆で、疑いを知らず、誠実だが、何より
愛されているのは、不運な人生を送り、最終的に敗北したためだ。輝かし
い軍功を収めたおかげで偉大な存在となるが、それゆえに、その後の失墜
はより印象的で人々の心を打った。義経の悲劇的な敗北は、敗者に対する
判官びいきの心情を生んだ。

■clan 一族　■naval 海軍の　■headed by ～が率いる　■ascendance to（権
力の座など）に就くこと　■competitor 競争相手　■take refuge with～に逃げ道
を求める　■upbringing 育ち　■sincere 誠実な　■misfortune 不運
■poignant 痛切な

18 Fujiwara no Teika
Classic Poet Master

Fujiwara no Sadaie is also known as Fujiwara no Teika. A poet and critic of classical *waka* poetry, Teika was one of the six **compilers** of the imperial **anthology** known as *Shin Kokinshu*, "New Collection from Ancient and Modern Times," completed in about 1205. He was also the collector of another anthology titled *Shinchokusenshu*, "New Imperial Collection."

Teika came from a **prominent** family of classical poets and became a favorite of the former Emperor Go-Toba, an **accomplished** poet and patron of the poets of his period. Teika and his **cohorts** conducted poetry meetings and contests in addition to gathering materials for imperial anthologies.

Succeeding his father as the head of the **foremost** family of court poets, Teika served as teacher of poetry to prominent figures including the shogun Minamoto no Sanetomo. He was appointed to one of the highest **bureaucratic** positions, and received a **directive** from Emperor Go-Horikawa to compile the "New Imperial Collection."

Separately, Teika made collections of his own poems and favorite poems by other poets, as models for his **pupils**. The most famous is *Hyakunin Isshu*, Single Poems by 100 Poets, a favorite among Japanese who used them in a game played at New Years.

Teika's **verses** often followed his father's **aesthetic** ideal of *yugen*, "mystery and depth." However, he developed his own ideal of *yoen*, "**ethereal** beauty," which **evoked** a magical atmosphere. The symbolic qualities of this ideal were conveyed by a technique known as *honkadori*, "**allusive** variation." This technique echoed a phrase or an image from a well-known poem in a new poem, adding depth to the new poem. (277)

藤原定家

和歌の達人

［1162-1241］

藤原定家とも呼ばれる定家は、歌人で批評家でもあり、6人の撰者の一人として、1205年頃に完成した『新古今和歌集』を編纂。さらに『新勅撰和歌集』も撰した。

和歌の歌人の名門に生まれた定家は後鳥羽上皇に寵愛される。上皇は秀でた歌人で、同時代の歌人らの後ろ盾にもなった。定家は他の歌人らと歌会や歌合を開き、勅撰集に収める歌も集めた。

父・俊成の跡を継いで宮廷の歌人として「歌の家」の当主となり、将軍・源実朝ら有力者にも和歌を指導。正二位・権中納言に任じられ、後堀河天皇の命を受けて『新勅撰和歌集』を編纂した。

また、弟子らの手本となるように、自作の歌や他の歌人が詠んだお気に入りの歌を集めた歌集も編纂。最も有名な『小倉百人一首』は日本人に好まれ、歌がるたとして正月の遊戯となった。

定家の歌は、父の美意識、幽玄を踏襲したものが多いが、定家は独自にこの世のものとは思えない魔境の美、妖艶と呼ばれるスタイルを極めていった。この美意識を象徴する特徴を伝えるのが本歌取と呼ばれる比喩表現で、これは、有名な歌の一節やイメージを取り入れ、新たな歌に膨らみを持たせる技法である。

■compiler 編纂者　■anthology 歌集　■prominent 有名な　■accomplished 熟達した　■cohort 仲間　■succeed 〜の後任となる　■foremost 主要な　■bureaucratic 官僚制度の　■directive 命令　■pupil 弟子　■verse 詩歌　■aesthetic 美的に優れた　■ethereal この世のものとは思えない　■evoke 呼び起こす　■allusive 比喩に富んだ

19 Shinran
Preacher to Everyone

A **disciple** of Honen, Shinran was also **banished** from the capital for preaching the **exclusive** practice of the *nenbutsu*. After Honen's death, Shinran found other disciples of Honen preaching their own interpretations of Honen's message. Preaching what he thought was Honen's true message, Shinran developed the Jodo Shin Sect, the "true essence of Pure Land Buddhism."

Shinran followed Honen in saying that wisdom is **unreachable** through the effort of the self, *jiriki*. He believed that wisdom comes only from the power of Amida. Therefore, one should trust completely in *tariki*, the powers of Amida Buddha. While Honen taught that one should **intone** the *nenbutsu* in order to **be reborn** in the Pure Land, Shinran taught that people are already saved because Amida vowed to save us. Therefore, we **recite** the *nenbutsu* as an act of **gratitude** for what we have already received.

Two beliefs promoted by Shinran changed Buddhism in Japan. One was his **abandonment** of **celibacy**. Shinran married and had seven children. Other priests had married, but Shinran was a pioneer in terms of religious **justification** for marrying. He also abandoned the **restriction against** eating fish and **fowl**.

Shinran's teachings brought considerable resistance from the **established** Buddhist authorities. Shinran **was exiled to** Echigo in northwestern Honshu. When Honen died, Shinran did not return to Kyoto, but traveled to the eastern provinces, preaching to people of all classes. **In accordance with** his wishes, no official government funeral was held when he died—a refusal even in death to **entrust** himself to the establishment.(253)

親鸞

あらゆる階級に説法

［1173-1262］

　法然（p.34）の弟子、親鸞もまた、専修念仏の教えを説いたことで都を追われた。法然の死後、他の弟子らが法然の教えを独自に解釈して説いていることを知った親鸞は、法然の真の教えと考えたものを説き、浄土真宗として発展させた。

　親鸞は法然に倣い、智慧は自力では得られず、阿弥陀如来の力でしか得られないため、阿弥陀仏の力、すなわち他力を本願すべきであると考えた。法然が浄土で生まれ変わるためには念仏を唱えなければならないと説いたのに対し、親鸞は、阿弥陀如来は私たちを救うと誓ってくださっているのだから、私たちはすでに救われている、したがって、すでに受け取ったことへの感謝の気持ちを表すために念仏を唱えるべきだと説いた。

　親鸞が推し進めた2つの思想は日本の仏教を変えた。ひとつは、親鸞が妻帯したことだ。親鸞は結婚して子どもを7人もうけている。それまでにも妻をめとっていた僧侶はいたが、親鸞は宗教上、婚姻を正当化した先駆けとなった。また、魚や家禽類を食べてはならないという戒律を破り、肉食を断行した。

　親鸞の教えは、仏教の主流派の権威からはかなりの抵抗に遭い、親鸞は本州北西部の越後（現・新潟）に配流された。法然が亡くなると、京には帰らずに関東に向かい、あらゆる階級の人々に説法した。亡くなったとき（最期は帰京して迎えた）は、親鸞の意向で幕府による公葬は行われなかった。これは死ぬ際も既存の権威にその身を委ねることを拒否したためである。

■disciple 弟子　■banish 追放する　■exclusive 唯一の　■unreachable 達し得ない　■intone 吟唱する　■be reborn 生まれ変わる　■recite 暗唱する　■gratitude 感謝　■abandonment 中止　■celibacy 宗教上の誓いによる禁欲主義　■justification 正当化　■restriction against ～に対する制限　■fowl 家禽類　■established 確立された　■be exiled to ～に追放される　■in accordance with ～に従って　■entrust 委ねる

20 Dogen
The Disciple of Seated Meditation

The priest Eisai traveled to Song China to study the roots of T'ien-t'ai Buddhism but instead discovered and studied the new Ch'an sect. After returning to Japan in 1191 he **propagated** the new religion, the Rinzai sect of Zen Buddhism. He encountered resistance from the T'ien-t'ai **clergy** in Kyoto. When he moved to Kamakura, however, he **found a ready audience** with the shogunate, which was independent of the culture of the capital area. He won protection from the shogunate and the **allegiance** of large numbers of warriors.

Following in Eisai's footsteps, Dogen studied on Mt. Hiei before going to Song China in 1223 and becoming an **adherent** of the Ch'an (Ts'ao-tung) school of Buddhism. When he returned to Japan in 1227, he established the Soto sect of Zen Buddhism. He began writing his masterpiece *Treasury of the True Dharma Eye (Shobogenzo)*, in which he **contended** that all people possess the potential to become a Buddha. Enlightenment is possible for anyone, if they just meditate in **the lotus position**. He called this *shikan taza*, "just sitting." He attempted to get approval from the imperial court to teach Zen, but T'ien-t'ai leaders chased him from his temple.

As a result, he departed from the capital city and established a **monastery** in far off Echizen, now Fukui Prefecture. The temple, Eiheiji, continues to be a major Zen training institution known for its **rigorous discipline**.

Dogen's introduction of seated meditation, or *zazen*, as the highest and best practice colored Buddhist practice in Japan significantly. It later spread around the world. (256)

道元

座禅の神髄を普及

［1200-1253］

　僧侶・栄西（日本に本格的な禅宗を持ち帰る）は、天台宗のルーツを学ぶために中国の宋に渡るが、そこで禅宗の新たな宗派を知って研究し、1191年に帰国後、禅宗の一派、臨済宗を布教する。京の天台宗の僧からは快く思われずに抵抗を受けたが、都の公家文化の影響を受けない鎌倉幕府には受け入れられ、幕府の庇護と多くの武士の支持を集めた。

　道元は栄西に倣い、比叡山で修行した後、1223年に宋に渡り、曹洞禅を学ぶ。1227年に帰国すると、禅宗の曹洞宗を開き、万人が成仏できるとする名著『正法眼蔵』の執筆に取り掛かる。蓮華座、すなわち結跏趺坐で瞑想すれば、誰でも悟りを開ける。道元はこの考えを、「ただひたすらに座る」ことを意味する只管打坐と呼んだ。道元は禅を教えるために朝廷の許可を得ようとしたが、天台宗の指導層に寺を追われた。

　そうして都を離れた道元は、遠い越前（現・福井）に僧院・永平寺を開いた。永平寺は今なお、厳しい修行で知られる禅の修行道場である。

　道元が最高・最良の修行として紹介した坐禅は、日本の仏道修行に大きな影響を与え、その後、世界中に広まっていった。

■propagate 広める　■clergy 僧職者　■find a ready audience 受容される
■allegiance 忠誠心　■adherent 信奉者　■contend 主張する　■the lotus
position 蓮華座　■monastery 僧院　■rigorous 厳格な　■discipline 修行

21 Emperor Go-Daigo
The Emperor Who Sought Direct Rule

In the late 13th century, Japan was governed by two institutions of power: the imperial court in Kyoto and the military bakufu in Kamakura. But in reality, almost all of the court's power had been taken by the bakufu. In the 1330s, however, due to conflict within the bakufu, its strength declined and Japan plunged into chaos.

Emperor Go-Daigo was the first to attempt to reestablish power. He wanted to weaken warrior dominance and restore political power to the imperial family. He attempted to form a coalition among people the bakufu had **alienated**. But the bakufu defeated his attempts to regain actual power. Go-Daigo fled Kyoto, was captured, and **was exiled to** the Oki Islands. Go-Daigo escaped in 1333 and gained the support of Ashikaga Takauji, who took on the role of the military ruler who protected the emperor.

Upon returning to Kyoto, Go-Daigo once again sought to restore a ruling imperial house in Kyoto under the Kenmu Restoration. Takauji meanwhile built a new shogunate headquarters in the Muromachi section of Kyoto. Other political and military leaders shifted **allegiance to** whichever party seemed to have the best **prospects**.

In 1336 the two main parties clashed. After several campaigns, Go-Daigo retreated to the mountains of Yoshino and, with his allies, formed the **so-called** "southern court." Dual imperial courts continued until 1392, when the shogun Ashikaga Yoshimitsu brought the current southern **pretender to the throne** back to Kyoto. Yoshimitsu agreed that the princes of the "southern court" and the "northern court" would take turns in succeeding to the imperial throne. But he did not keep his promise. By 1408, Yoshimitsu himself had **virtually all** of the powers of the emperor. (268)

後醍醐天皇

親政をめざした天皇

［1288-1339］

　13世紀後半の日本は、権力を持つ二つの機関、京の朝廷と鎌倉幕府によって統治されていたが、朝廷は幕府に実権をほぼ奪われた状態であった。しかし1330年代になると、内部争いなどで幕府の権威が低下し、日本は混乱を極めていく。

　最初に立て直しを試みたのは後醍醐天皇だ。後醍醐天皇は倒幕と天皇親政を望み、幕府に疎まれていた諸国の武士らを味方につけ、実権を取り戻そうとした試みは、幕府にくじかれる。京都から逃れたところ、捕らえられて隠岐島に流された。1333年には隠岐島を脱出し、足利尊氏を味方につけた（鎌倉幕府倒幕）。尊氏は後醍醐天皇を守り、軍政を司る役目（鎮守府将軍）を得た。

　京に帰還した後醍醐天皇は、建武の新政によって京で天皇を中心とした政治体制を再び試みるものの（武士の不満を招き）、離反した尊氏は京に室町幕府を開き、政治に関わる指導層や武将らは、最も有望と思える側に鞍替えした。

　1336年、後醍醐天皇側と尊氏側が衝突。後醍醐天皇は尊氏討伐を何度か試みるが、吉野の山に退き、味方とともにいわゆる南朝を開く。尊氏が別に立てた天皇（北朝）とともに二つの朝廷が並立したこの南北朝時代は、1392年に将軍・足利義満が京で南北朝合体を果たすまで続くこととなる。義満は、南朝と北朝の皇子を交替で天皇にすることを約束したが、その約束は反故にされ、1408年まで、義満自身が天皇に代わってほぼ全権を握り続けた。

■alienate 遠ざける　■be exiled to 〜に追放される　■allegiance to 〜への忠誠
■prospect 成功する見込み　■so-called いわゆる　■pretender to the throne
自分が王位・皇位継承者だと主張する人　■virtually all ほぼすべての

22 Zeami
Creative Master of Noh

Among the significant artists who **received patronage from** Ashikaga Yoshimitsu were the actor-playwrights Kan'ami and his son Zeami. These two creative **geniuses** were primarily responsible for combining *sarugaku* dance, music, masks, and storytelling and developing it into Noh drama.

As playwrights, they took stories from older sources such as *The Tale of the Heike*, **tales of court life** including *The Tale of Genji*, Buddhist **moral tales**, and collections of narratives. The father and son then turned these tales into dramatic art which possessed great aesthetic and psychological depth.

Their creative genius became widely known. The father and son **gained access to** the highest circles of Kyoto society. Thanks to this, they learned how to appeal to highly sophisticated tastes, and that raised the level of their performances.

Upon Kan'ami's death, Zeami **succeeded to** the leadership of the Kanze **troupe** of performers. At the end of his career, Zeami began to compose *Fushi Kaden, The Transmission of the Flower of Acting Style,* to convey the art of Noh to following generations. This superb work is considered the **quintessential** work of art theory of that period of Japanese history and the **fundamental basis** for Noh drama. Fortunately, it is translated into English as well. (202)

世阿弥

能を大成させた立役者

[1363?-1443?]

　足利義満（室町幕府3代将軍）の庇護を受けた大変優れた芸術家に、能役者にして能作者の観阿弥と息子の世阿弥がいる。**天才的**なクリエイターだった2人は、まず猿楽、曲舞の音曲、面、物語を融合して能楽劇として大成させた。

　観阿弥と世阿弥は能作者として、『平家物語』や、『源氏物語』などの宮廷物語、仏教説話、さまざまな物語などの古い素材を典拠として物語を創作。そうした物語を美的にも精神的にも深みを持つ演劇芸術に高めた。

　父子の創造的な才能は広く知られるようになり、2人は京の貴族社会に出入りするようになる。そのおかげで上流階級の非常に洗練された嗜好に訴える術を身に付け、能楽のレベルを高めていった。

　観阿弥の死後、世阿弥は観世一座の大夫（長）を引き継いだ。晩年には、能の芸を後世に伝えるために『風姿花伝』を書き進めた。この秀作は、当時の日本における芸術論の**神髄**を表しており、能楽の**基礎**とされている。幸いなことに英訳もされている。

■ receive patronage from 〜の庇護を得る　■ genius 天才、才能　■ tale of court life 宮廷生活の話　■ moral tale 説話　■ gain access to 〜に接近する ■ succeed to 〜を引き継ぐ　■ troupe 一座　■ quintessential 神髄の ■ fundamental basis 基本的原理

23 Ashikaga Yoshimasa
Patron of Higashiyama Culture

In 1449, just prior to the Onin War, a ten-year period that destroyed most of the Kyoto capital, Ashikaga Yoshimasa became shogun. Clearly not **cut out to be** a military leader, **much less** a shogun, Yoshimasa did his best to surrender his official duties and **devote himself to** more pleasurable interests. In 1473, he transferred the office of shogun to his son, and a few years after the Onin War, he **commenced** construction of a **retreat** for his own use. It was called Ginkakuji, the Silver Pavilion, and it is still in existence in the eastern hills of Kyoto, the district known as Higashiyama.

During the earlier Kitayama period, Kinkakuji, the Golden Pavilion, had served as the heart of a **sophisticated** culture with Noh theater at its core. During the Higashiyama period, Yoshimasa's Silver Pavilion became a center for renga, a form of linked verses composed by an **assembly** of poets. The elegant villa and the garden Yoshimasa had created became one of the most representative examples of Japanese aesthetics. Yoshimasa's **patronage** of the tea ceremony also awakened a new interest in tea implements, lacquer ware (*maki-e*), architecture, garden design, and flower arrangement.

Through Yoshimasa and the people who gathered around him, Higashiyama culture promoted *yugen* and *wabi*, the aura of mystery, **spareness**, **understatement**, and **rustic** ideals that became the highest aesthetic elements of Japanese culture.(226)

足利義政

東山文化の後援者
[1436-1490]

　応仁の乱に先立つ1449年、足利義政は将軍となるが、応仁の乱は約10年に及び、京の大半が戦乱で荒廃した。義政は武将のリーダー、ましてや将軍には不向きで、政務に意欲を失い、趣味の世界に没頭した。1473年、将軍職を息子に譲り、応仁の乱終結から数年後、自身の隠居所の建設に着手する。銀閣寺と呼ばれるこの山荘は、京都の東山区に現存している。

　これより前の北山文化時代には金閣寺が洗練された文化の中心地となり、能が大成されるが、この東山文化時代の中心となるのは義政の銀閣寺で、複数の歌人が歌を連ねて詠む連歌が花開く。義政が造った優雅な山荘と庭園は日本の美意識の代表例の一つとなり、また、義政が茶道に傾倒したために、茶道具、蒔絵、建築、作庭、生け花などに対する新たな関心を呼び覚ました。

　義政およびその周りに集まった人々を通じ、東山文化によって幽玄枯淡、侘びなど、その後の日本文化における最も美意識の高い価値観が育まれていった。

■ cut out to be ～に向いている　■ much less まして～でない　■ devote oneself to ～に熱中する　■ commence 開始する　■ retreat 隠遁所　■ sophisticated 洗練された　■ assembly 集まり　■ patronage 愛顧　■ spareness 乏しさ　■ understatement 控えめさ　■ rustic 質朴な

24 Sen no Rikyu
The Tea Master

Two men who sought to unify Japan during the medieval period, Oda Nobunaga and Toyotomi Hideyoshi, are known for their military and political power. But the Azuchi-Momoyama period in which they were active was also important for its culture. It is especially known for the development of the tea ceremony. Major **feudal lords competed in showing off** their elegant tea bowls, tea houses, and knowledge of tea and tea implements. Perhaps the greatest of the tea masters was Sen no Rikyu. Rikyu studied both the tea ceremony and Zen Buddhism before becoming serving as *sado*, the tea ceremony **officiant** for the two military chiefs who were gradually uniting the country: Nobunaga and Hideyoshi.

Sen no Rikyu was a merchant in the port of Sakai who developed the highest ideals of *wabicha*. This style of tea ceremony involved a small group of people gathered in a small, **sparely decorated** room especially designed for such gatherings. The room, implements, and process stressed a **rustic** and simple event. The host prepared and served the tea, using pottery and utensils of simple design.

The ritual was **minimal**, but the tea ceremony was ultimately an activity for elites. Rikyu's taste was superb. He selected flower holders created from bamboo and often used **rough** black raku ware teabowls. He preferred to use what was easily available in order to emphasize the ordinary, everyday elements in the tea ceremony.

Rikyu and Hideyoshi were considered close **acquaintances**, but as a result of some **discord** between them, Hideyoshi issued an order for Rikyu to **commit** seppuku, **ritual suicide**. (254)

千利休

茶の湯を大成

[1522-1591]

　中世日本で天下統一をめざした織田信長（p.58）と豊臣秀吉（p.60）は、軍事力と政治力で名を馳せたが、2人が活躍した安土桃山時代は、文化面でも重要な役割を果たし、特に茶の湯が発展したことで知られている。この時代、主だった**大名**は、優美な茶碗や茶室、茶や茶道具に関する知識を**披露して競い合った**。茶人の大家といえるのが千利休だ。利休は、茶の湯と禅宗を学び、天下統一を推し進めていた2人の武将、信長と秀吉に茶頭として仕えた。

　利休は堺の港の商人で、（精神的な深みを味わうという）侘び茶の崇高な理想を極めた。利休が完成した茶の湯の様式は、茶会のために特別に設計された狭くて**簡素な**茶室に少人数で集まるといったもので、茶室、茶道具、作法も、茶会の**質朴とした簡素さ**を際立たせ、茶会の主人はシンプルなデザインの茶器や道具で茶を立てて出した。

　茶の湯のまるで儀式のような作法は**最小限**ではあったが、侘び茶はやがて特権階級のものとなる。利休は美的感覚に優れ、竹製の花器を選び、**歪**んだ黒楽茶碗を用いることが多かった。茶の湯においてありふれた日常の要素を強調するため、手近で入手できるものを使うことを好んだ。

　秀吉とは親しい**仲**であったが、やがて**軋轢**が生じ、**切腹**を命じられた。

■ feudal lord 大名　　■ compete in 〜で競う　　■ show off 〜を誇示する
■ officiant（祭式などの）施行者　　■ sparely decorated あまり装飾されていない
■ rustic 飾り気のない　　■ minimal 最小限の　　■ rough でこぼこの
■ acquaintance 知人　　■ discord 仲違い　　■ commit ritual suicide 切腹する

25 Oda Nobunaga

Ambition for Total Power

The first of three unifiers of the country, Oda Nobunaga was the son of a deputy military governor of Owari domain. When his father died, he quickly seized power and fought off all **contenders** for control of the domain.

Early on in his career, Nobunaga purchased more than 1,000 new **harquebuses** introduced by the Europeans. With these weapons, he **revolutionized** Japanese warfare. He trained ordinary soldiers—not samurai—to load and fire their weapons as fast as possible. Because it took time to reload, he had them line up in ranks, so that they could fire **sequentially**. One rank fired while the next rank reloaded, giving the enemy no chance to **counter-attack**.

This new **strategy** proved decisive at the Battle of Nagashino in 1575. Nobunaga's army, including 3,000 men with **muskets**, **routed** a force of samurai on horseback. Recognizing the superiority of his ordinary fighting men with weapons, other daimyo soon adopted his strategy.

Nobunaga's willingness to destroy anyone who opposed him **extended to** the armed Buddhists of the Ishiyama Honganji. He then **gained notoriety for** attacking Enryakuji on Mt. Hiei in 1571. His troops surrounded the entire mountain, burned every building, and killed every single **inhabitant**. With such **ruthless** measures, he pursued an ambitious campaign to unify the whole country.

His method was to **eliminate** rivals, take their land, and give it to those who were loyal to him. By the time he was **assassinated** in 1582, by one of his own allies, he had gained control of almost one third of Japan. (254)

織田信長

権力を掌握した野心家

［1534-1582］

　天下統一を目指した 3 人のうちのひとり目、織田信長は、尾張国の守護
代の家臣・信秀の息子。父が亡くなると、直ちに権力を掌握しようと、尾
張国の支配権を争う者たちを蹴散らした。

　頭角を現した信長は、欧州人がもたらした1,000丁以上の新型の**火縄銃**を
購入し、この銃器で日本の戦法に**革命を起こした**。信長は、武士ではなく
足軽を訓練し、できるだけ早く火薬を装填して銃を発射させた。火薬を再
装填するのには時間がかかるため、足軽兵を列に並ばせて布陣し、**連続し
て発砲**できるようにしたのである。（一説には）1 列目が発砲する間に、
次の列が火薬を詰め直し、敵に**反撃**するチャンスを与えなかったとされる。

　この新**戦略**は、1575年の長篠合戦で勝利の決め手となった。**鉄砲**を携え
た3,000人の兵がいる信長軍は、（武田勝頼側の）騎馬隊に**圧勝**。武器を備
えた足軽兵が刀を持つ武士を上回ることを認識した他の大名たちも、すぐ
に信長の戦略を取り入れるようになった。

　自分に歯向かう者をたたきのめす信長の姿勢は、石山本願寺の武装した
僧侶や信徒らにも**向けられ**、さらに信長は1571年に比叡山延 暦 寺をも焼
き打ちして**悪名をとどろかせる**。このとき信長は、比叡山全体を包囲し、
建物をすべて焼き払い、僧侶はもちろん、**住民**らを皆殺しにしたとされる。
こうした**容赦**のない手段で、信長は天下を統一する野心的な作戦を展開し
ていった。

　信長は、敵対する相手を殺して土地を奪い、自分に忠実な配下にその土
地を与える方法を取り、1582年に側近の一人に**暗殺**されるまで、日本の 3
分の 1 近くを支配下に収めた。

■ contender 競争相手　■ harquebus 火縄銃　■ revolutionize 革命を起こす
■ sequentially 連続して　■ counter-attack 反撃する　■ strategy 戦略
■ muskets マスケット銃　■ rout 圧勝する　■ extend to ～に広がる
■ gain notoriety for ～で悪評を得る　■ inhabitant 住民　■ ruthless 無慈悲な
■ eliminate 抹殺する　■ assassinate 暗殺する

26 Toyotomi Hideyoshi
Unifier and Suppressor

The second unifier, Toyotomi Hideyoshi, **elected** a policy of building **alliances**. Although he attacked those who resisted, he was willing to accept military lords who shifted alliances and joined his side. Through building alliances, he was able to gain control of virtually all of Japan by 1590.

Hideyoshi systematized many of Nobunaga's ideas. He **instituted** so-called "sword hunts" as a means of **disarming** peasants and separating the warriors from the peasants. To strengthen his control over his allies, he required that they offer **hostages** in order to ensure their loyalty. He also turned against the **Jesuit** missionaries who had arrived in the 1550s and succeeded in winning **converts** in southern domains. The anti-Christian **edicts** he issued were not always **enforced**, but he started the trend toward opposing this foreign religion. He ordered Christian **missionaries** out of Japan in 1587.

Within the next decade, he **became obsessed with** the possibility that daimyo and commoners who converted to Christianity might not be loyal to him. Missionaries were increasingly **persecuted**, and in 1596, he had 26 Franciscan and Jesuit missionaries and Japanese followers **crucified** in Nagasaki. This was a first step toward complete suppression of Christianity decades later.

Hideyoshi launched two massive campaigns to take over Korea in 1592 and 1597, but neither succeeded. When he returned to Japan, he brought back communities of **potters**, who settled in Japan and produced superior wares in Hagi, Arita, and Satsuma. (234)

豊臣秀吉

抑圧者の顔をもつ天下人

[1537-1598]

　天下統一を目指す2人目となる豊臣秀吉（とよとみひでよし）は、同盟関係を築く方針を採用し、抵抗する相手を攻撃する一方で、自分の側に寝返った武将のことは快く受け入れた。そうした同盟を活用することで、1590年までに日本全国をほぼ掌握した。

　秀吉は（織田）信長（のぶなが）（p.58）の構想の多くを体系化。農民から**武器を没収**して兵農分離を推し進めるために「刀狩（かたながり）」を**制定**し、さらに、同盟を結んだ大名に対する支配力を強めるため、忠誠の証しとして**人質**を差し出させた。また、1550年代に日本にやってきて、九州の藩で**改宗者**を増やしていた**イエズス会の宣教師**と敵対するようになった。キリスト教に反対する秀吉の**命令**は必ずしも**施行**されたわけではなかったが、やがて秀吉は、キリスト教を弾圧するようになり、1587年にはバテレン（宣教師）追放令を発布した。

　それからの10年間、秀吉は、キリスト教に改宗した大名や庶民が自分に歯向かうのではないかという強迫観念にとらわれるようになり、宣教師への**迫害を強め**、1596年にはフランシスコ会員とイエズス会の宣教師、日本人信者の26人を長崎で**十字架**にはりつけにした。これが始まりとなり、数十年後にはキリスト教は徹底的に弾圧されるようになった。

　秀吉は1592年と1597年に朝鮮を服属させるために朝鮮出兵を大々的に開始するが、いずれも不首尾に終わった。このとき朝鮮から連れ帰られた陶工（とうこう）は日本に定住し、萩（はぎ）、有田（ありた）、薩摩（さつま）で優れた焼き物を生産した。

■ elect 選ぶ　■ alliance 同盟　■ institute 制定する　■ disarm 武装解除する
■ hostage 人質　■ Jesuit イエズス会士　■ convert 改宗者　■ edict 命令
■ enforce 施行する　■ missionary 宣教師　■ become obsessed with 〜に取りつかれる　■ persecute 迫害する　■ crucify（十字架に人を）はりつけにする
■ potter 陶工

27 Tokugawa Ieyasu
The Ultimate Unifier

Matsudaira Takechiyo spent his youth held **captive** by his father's ene-
mies, then was forced to serve as a **hostage** to his father's allies. In 1561 he finally became independent and took control of his father's **domains** in Okazaki, near
present-day Nagoya. After **allying himself with** Oda Nobunaga, he took the
name Ieyasu and the ancient family name Tokugawa.

Combined Oda and Tokugawa forces defeated rivals, giving Ieyasu a
strategic position in central Japan. Ieyasu then formed an alliance with Nobunaga's
successor, Toyotomi Hideyoshi, and they began unifying the Kanto Plain.
Hideyoshi assigned Ieyasu to a strategically and **fiscally** disadvantaged domain in
the Kanto Plain with headquarters in a fishing village called Edo. It seemed like
a **demotion** to Ieyasu initially, but he gradually realized that it was a potentially
productive and **geographically** unified region.

Before Hideyoshi died in 1598, he had Ieyasu and his other generals
agree to serve his very young son Hideyori. But in 1600, Ieyasu went to war
against the anti-Tokugawa forces in a battle at Sekigahara and easily won.

Ieyasu was given the title of *shogun* in 1603, and began **consolidating**
rule over the entire country. He established control over Kyoto and **claimed authority over** all Japanese feudal lords (*daimyo*). His achievement was to bring an
unprecedented unity and a succession stable enough to last for generations.
Luck played a part in his success, but he laid the foundation for administration
of the entire country, started Edo on the path to becoming the world city of
Tokyo, and **initiated** a peace that continued for two and a half centuries. (263)

徳川家康

太平をもたらした最終的な天下人

[1542-1616]

　松平竹千代（幼名）は幼い頃に父と敵対する勢力に捕らえられ、その後、（捕虜交換により）父の味方側・今川家の人質として過ごすことを余儀なくされた。1561年、ついに今川から離反し、現・名古屋に近い岡崎にあった父の領地を掌握。織田信長（p.58）と同盟を結んだ後、名を家康、姓も松平氏の源流とされる徳川へと改めた。

　徳川軍は織田軍とともに対立する大名らを次々撃破し、家康は中部日本で戦略的な拠点を築く。その後、信長の後継者である豊臣秀吉（p.60）と同盟を結び、ともに関東平野の天下統一に乗り出した。家康は秀吉に、戦略的にも財政的にも不利な関東平野の漁村、江戸への転封を命じられ、当初は降格にも思えたが、次第に江戸に潜在的に備わった生産性と地理的な統一感に気付くようになる。

　秀吉は1598年に亡くなる前、家康をはじめとする武将らに対して、まだ非常に幼い息子の秀頼に仕えることを承諾させた。しかし1600年、家康は関ヶ原の戦いで反家康勢力と戦い、大勝した。

　家康は1603年、征夷大将軍に任じられ、（幕府を開き）天下を統一していった。京都の朝廷に対する武家の権威を確立（禁中並公家諸法度）し、諸大名を統制（武家諸法度）した。家康の業績は、かつてない（完全な）統一と、何世代も続く安定した継承をもたらしたことだ。運にも恵まれながら家康は国政の礎を築き、江戸が世界都市・東京に発展する道を開いて約250年間にわたって続く太平の世の始まりを実現した。

■captive 捕虜になった　■hostage 人質　■domain 領地　■ally oneself with 〜と同盟する　■fiscally 財政的に　■demotion 降格　■productive 生産的な　■geographically 地理的に　■consolidate（権力などを）固める　■claim authority over 〜に対する支配権を主張する　■unprecedented 前例のない　■initiate 開始する

28 Hosokawa Gracia
More than a Loyal Wife

The **vicissitudes** of the life of Hosokawa Tama involved all three of the unifiers of Japan, at least indirectly.

To begin with, she was one of the daughters of Akechi Mitsuhide, who rose up against his lord Oda Nobunaga in the Honnoji Incident. Although she had nothing to do with her father's plot against the powerful Nobunaga, it would have been normal to **find** her **guilty** by **mere association**. However, her husband Hosokawa Tadaoki refused to assist Akechi's plans, and she survived one **close call**.

Two years later Toyotomi Hideyoshi, the second of the unifying figures in Japan, allowed her to **take up residence in** Osaka. During this period, she became a Christian and received the **baptismal name** Gracia. This occurred during the period in which Christian missionaries and Japanese converts to the religion were not yet suppressed by the government.

In 1598, as the **political tide** changed once again, her husband Tadaoki **sided with** the third unifier, Tokugawa Ieyasu. Tadaoki left somewhat **startling** instructions with the senior **retainer** of his family, whose name was Ogasawara Shosai. Tadaoki ordered Ogasawara to **execute** her if Ieyasu's chief rival, Ishida Mitsunari, ever attempted to seize her and take her as a hostage. When Mitsunari actually did attempt to capture her, Ogasawara followed his lord's instructions and executed her, before committing suicide himself.

Hosokawa Gracia is, as a result of this series of dramatic **encounters**, often held up as a model of the virtuous samurai wife. (243)

細川ガラシャ

気高き武士の妻の鑑

［1563-1600］

　細川たま（ガラシャ）の波瀾万丈の人生には、間接的にではあるが、天下統一を目指した3人の武将全員が関わっている。

　まず、父は、本能寺の変で主君・織田信長（p.58）に謀反を起こした明智光秀だ。たまは、強大な権力を持っていた信長への父の謀反には関与していなかったが、当時は肉親というだけで連座に問われるのが普通だった。だが、夫の細川忠興が光秀の計画に協力することを拒んだため、たまは間一髪で難を逃れた。

　2年後、信長の跡を継いだ豊臣秀吉（p.60）に許され、たまは大坂に居を構えることを許された。この時期、たまはキリスト教に改宗し、ガラシャという洗礼名を授かる。キリスト教の宣教師や日本人の改宗者が幕府から弾圧されるようになる前のことだ。

　1598年、再び政情が変わり、夫・忠興は天下統一を目指す徳川家康側に付く。忠興は、家老の小笠原少斎（小笠原秀清）に思いがけない指示を与えていた。家康と対立していた石田三成方にガラシャが人質に取られそうになった場合は、（キリスト教の教えで自殺ができない）ガラシャを殺すように命じていたのだ。その後、実際、三成がガラシャを捕らえようとすると、少斎は主君の命令に従ってガラシャを介錯し、自害した。

　このようにドラマチックな出会いに次々に翻弄された細川ガラシャは、しばしば、貞淑な武士の妻の鑑とされた。

■ vicisitude 浮き沈み　　■ find〜guilty 〜を有罪と見なす　　■ mere ほんの　■ association 付き合い　■ close call 危機一髪　■ take up residence in 〜に居を定める　■ baptismal name 洗礼名　■ political tide 政治的形勢　■ side with 〜の側に付く　■ startling 衝撃的な　　■ retainer 家臣　■ execute 処刑する　■ encounter 出会い

Chapter 2

近世

Pre-modern Period

Ichikawa Danjuro I

Hasekura Tsunenaga

Kobori Enshu

Chikamatsu Monzaemon

Motoori Norinaga

Yamada Nagamasa

Tokugawa Yoshimune

Honda Toshiaki

Ino Tadataka

Tsutaya Juzaburo

Daikokuya Kodayu

Utagawa Hiroshige

Toshusai Sharaku

Jippensha Ikku

John Manjiro

Sakamoto Ryoma

Yoshida Shoin

29 Hasekura Tsunenaga
Would-be Diplomat to Europe

Under orders from the daimyo Date Masamune, and with the permission of Tokugawa Ieyasu, in 1613 a **galleon** named the *San Juan Baptista* **set sail from** the north coast of Honshu bound **for** Europe. Aboard it was Hasekura Rokuemon Tsunenaga, who carried a letter from Masamune to the Spanish **monarch** asking for an agreement to establish trade. Another letter was addressed to Pope Paul V in Rome asking for more missionaries to be sent to Japan. Several foreign priests accompanied the mission as **interpreters**, including Luis Sotelo.

The ship crossed the Pacific, landing once in California and then in Acapulco. Tsunenaga and his party **transited** New Spain on foot and donkey to Veracruz. From there they went by ship to Havana and on to Spain, where they landed on the southern coast. They met with King Philip III, who did not agree to a trade treaty, and then they **pressed on to** Rome. They reached Rome and on November 3, 1615, Hasekura met Pope Paul V and **presented** Date's letter.

The return journey passed through Mexico, Manila, and Nagasaki on the way back to Sendai, where they arrived in 1620. It was an **arduous** seven-year journey. Unfortunately, during those years the Tokugama shogunate's policies had changed dramatically.

When Hasekura left Japan, both Date and the Tokugawa **regime** were interested in Western culture and trade. But when he returned Christianity was being **suppressed** and foreign trade was becoming **restricted**. It was a tragic ending, but an **astounding** successful attempt to reach America and Europe, and return safely. (256)

支倉常長

悲劇のヨーロッパ派遣使節

[1571-1622]

　大名・伊達政宗（仙台藩主）の命と、徳川家康（p.62）の許可を受け、1613年にサン・フアン・バウティスタ号というガレオン船（帆船）が本州北岸からヨーロッパに向けて出航した。乗船していたのは支倉六右衛門長経（常長の初名）。政宗がスペイン国王（フェリペ3世）に通商を求める書状と、ローマ教皇パウロ5世に宣教師をもっと派遣してほしいと訴える書状を携えていた。ルイス・ソテロをはじめ、フランシスコ会の宣教師も数人、通訳として同行した。

　船は太平洋を横断し、いったんカリフォルニアに上陸した後、メキシコのアカプルコに上陸。常長一行は、徒歩とロバでヌエバ・エスパーニャ副王領を横断し、大西洋岸のベラクルスにたどり着く。そこから船でハバナに向かい、スペインの南海岸に上陸した。フェリペ3世に謁見したものの、通商条約への同意は得られず、その後、一行はローマを目指して前進。ローマに到着した常長は1615年11月3日、教皇パウロ5世に拝謁し、政宗の書状を奉呈した。

　帰途はメキシコ、マニラ、長崎を経由し、1620年に仙台に戻った。7年間の困難な旅だった。だが残念なことに、その間に徳川幕府の政策は劇的に変わっていた。

　常長が日本をたったときは、政宗も徳川幕府も西洋文化や貿易に関心を寄せていたが、帰国してみると、キリスト教は弾圧され、外国との貿易も制限されるようになっていた。悲劇的な結末ではあったが、常長がアメリカとヨーロッパにたどり着き、無事に帰国したことは、特筆すべき業績だ。

■ galleon ガレオン船　■ set sail from … for …から〜に向けて出帆する　■ monarch 君主　■ interpreter 通訳　■ transit 通過する　■ press on to 〜を目指して前進する　■ present 贈呈する　■ arduous 大変な　■ regime 政権　■ suppress 抑圧する　■ restrict 制限する　■ astounding 驚くべき

30 Kobori Enshu
Architect and Connoisseur

Son of the **commissioner** of public works (*sakuji bugyo*) under Toyotomi Hideyoshi, Kobori Enshu **followed in his father's footsteps** under the first three Tokugawa shoguns. Enshu is known as **a Renaissance man**, who was prominent as a tea master, a **connoisseur** of pottery, a garden designer, an architect, a **calligrapher**, and a poet.

As *sakuji bugyo*, **superintendent** of construction work, for the Tokugawa shogunate, his influence was enormous in the building of Fushimi Castle and Nijo Castle. Fushimi Castle was built as a retirement home by Toyotomi Hideyoshi in the Momoyama district of Kyoto, but was torn down by Tokugawa Iemitsu. Enshu created the garden at Ninomaru of Edo Castle which served as the headquarters of the Tokugawa Shogunate for over two centuries, until a series of fires in the 1860s destroyed the main **building complexes**.

As a young man, he studied the tea ceremony under Furuta Oribe and eventually founded his own school of tea, Enshu-ryu. He **was tasked with** instructing the third shogun, Tokugawa Iemitsu, in the ways of the tea ceremony. He was also active in **appraising** tea wares and was an important patron of ceramic production and excelled at garden design, a field in which he created some of the highly appreciated masterpieces in the country. Only a few of these gardens remain, but among them are the Konchiin sub-temple of the Nanzenji and the Kohoan sub-temple of the Daitokuji. (235)

小堀遠州

建築、作庭にセンスを発揮

[1579-1647]

　小堀遠州（政一）は、豊臣秀吉（p.60）に仕えた作事奉行の父の跡を継ぎ、徳川将軍に初代から3代続けて仕えた。**革新的な教養人**として知られ、傑出した茶人であった遠州は、茶器**鑑定**、作庭、建築、書、和歌に優れた才能を示した。

　徳川幕府の建設作業を**統括**する作事奉行としては、伏見城、二条城などの普請に多大な影響を与えた。伏見城は豊臣秀吉が京の桃山に隠居所として建てた屋敷だが、（3代将軍）徳川家光によって廃城となる。また、遠州が二の丸の庭を造成した江戸城は200年以上にわたって徳川幕府の拠点として機能していたが、1860年代に火災が相次ぎ、**本丸御殿**は焼失した。

　若き日の遠州は茶道を古田織部に師事し、遠州流茶道の開祖となる。3代将軍・徳川家光の下では、将軍家茶の湯指南に**任じられ**た。また、茶道具の**鑑定**も積極的に行い、焼き物生産の重要な後ろ盾となったとされる。作庭にも優れていたため、日本の名園のいくつかを造営。現存している庭園は少ないが、南禅寺金地院庭園や大徳寺孤篷庵などに見ることができる。

■ commissioner　長官　■ follow in one's footsteps　〜の跡を継ぐ　■ a Renaissance man　ルネサンス的教養人　■ connoisseur　目利き　■ calligrapher　書道　■ superintendent　最高責任者　■ building complex　複合建築群　■ be tasked with　〜を任される　■ appraise　鑑定する

31 Miyamoto Musashi

Swordsman Extraordinaire

At the Battle of Sekigahara in 1600, the feudal lords who joined the side of Tokugawa Ieyasu **were rewarded**, and the samurai who served these lords also **benefitted**. The samurai serving the feudal lords on the losing side, however, lost the source of their position and their income. Among the samurai on the losing side who became a *ronin*, "a masterless samurai," was Miyamoto Musashi.

Musashi **made a name for himself** by developing a two-sword style of fencing, known as *nito-ryu*, and used his considerable skills in defeating challengers. According to some accounts, he was **victorious** in more than 60 sword fights as he traveled extensively around Japan.

In 1638 he fought on the side of the Tokugawa shogunate during the **suppression** of the Shimabara Rebellion. Several years later he became an instructor in **swordsmanship** for the Hosokawa feudal lord in Kumamoto.

His philosophy of swordsmanship called "the Book of Five Rings" (*Gorin no sho*) is said to have been transmitted to a **disciple** at the end of his life.

Musashi's accomplishments have been **taken up in** popular literature, movies, a Kabuki play, and manga. The novel *Miyamoto Musashi* by Yoshikawa Eiji, based on Musashi's adventures, portrayed Musashi as a **seeker** for truth through the mastery of the sword and Zen training. It is difficult to know where the reality and legend separate, but he is a fascinating figure from the days when samurai were actually warriors. (237)

宮本武蔵

無二の剣豪

[1584-1645]

　1600年の関ヶ原の戦いでは、徳川家康（p.62）側に付いた大名が報われ、その大名に仕えた武士らも恩恵を受けた。一方、敗北した大名に仕えていた武士らは、それまでの地位と収入源を失った。そうした武士の中で浪人となった一人が、宮本武蔵であるとされている。

　武蔵は二刀流と呼ばれる剣術を極めて名を馳せ、技を駆使して相手を打ち負かした。複数の記録によれば、全国をくまなく巡って60回以上の剣の勝負に勝利したといわれている。

　1638年、島原の乱の鎮圧の際には武蔵は徳川幕府側に付いて出陣。数年後、熊本の細川藩主の兵法指南となった。

　剣術の奥義をまとめた『五輪書』は、晩年に弟子に伝えられたといわれている。

　武蔵の業績は、大衆文学、映画、歌舞伎、漫画などで取り上げられてきた。吉川英治の『宮本武蔵』は武蔵の冒険譚で、武蔵は剣の熟達と禅の修行を通じた真理の探求者として描かれている。事実と伝説的逸話の境目を見分けるのは難しいが、侍が本物の武士だった時代の魅力的な人物である。

■be rewarded 報酬を受ける　■be benefitted 利益を与えられる　■make a name for oneself 名を成す　■victorious 勝利した　■suppression 鎮圧
■swordsmanship 剣術　■disciple 弟子　■take up … in …を〜で取り上げる
■seeker 探求者

32 Ikenobo Senko II
Flowers with Deep Meaning

Flower offerings were a Buddhist ritual introduced to Japan early in the 7th century, perhaps by Ono no Imoko, one of Prince Shotoku's earliest **envoys** to China. He took residence at a small temple by a pond known as Rokkakudo, but the **hermitage** later became known as Ikenobo, literally, "a priest's residence by a pond."

The Japanese developed the arranging of flowers into an art form. Courtiers were already highly sensitive to flowers but in the fifteenth century, flower offerings developed into a distinctive art form with different styles and **schools**. In 1462, a T'ien-t'ai Buddhist monk named Senkei created a complex, **free-standing** vase arrangement called *rikka*, "standing flowers," and he became the first head of Ikenobo, the oldest school of flower arrangement (*ikebana*).

Two Ikenobo masters, Senko I and Senko II, completed the rikka style during the Azuchi-Momoyama period. Emperor Go-Mizunoo kept pace with the cultural developments in the capital and he began studying with Senko II, whose arrangements were even more sculptural than those of his **predecessors**. Over the next five years, Senko II, who was of **commoner status**, was invited by the emperor to serve as a judge in flower-arranging competitions.

Illustrated handscrolls, surviving to the present day show **asymmetric** arrangements, each with a grouping of seven branches, which serve as symbols of the **Buddhist cosmic idea of Sumeru**, *shumisen*, which has seven mountain walls. A second, less formal, style developed that was known as *nageirebana*, used for the *zashiki*. This style was favored by the **townspeople**, because it presented the natural beauty of flowers without complicated rules. (262)

池坊専好（2代）

生け花を高尚な芸術として確立

［1575?-1658］

　7世紀初めに仏前供花の風習が日本に伝わった。伝えたのはおそらく、聖徳太子（p.12）に登用された最初の遣隋使の一人、小野妹子だとされる。（出家した）妹子は、池のほとりにあった六角堂と呼ばれる小さな寺で暮らし、その僧坊は「池のそばの僧侶の住まい」を意味する「池坊」と呼ばれるようになった。

　日本人は生け花を芸術として発展させていった。宮廷に仕える人々はそれまでにも花に対する優れた感受性を持っていたが、15世紀になると、生け花は独自の芸術へと進化し、さまざまな様式や流派が生まれていった。1462年には、天台宗の僧、専慶が器を使って支えなしで花を立てる複雑な「立花」と呼ばれる様式を生み出し、最も古い華道の流派、池坊の始祖となった。

　安土桃山時代に立花を大成させたのが、初代・池坊専好、2代目・専好という2人の池坊の家元である。後水尾天皇は、京で文化が発展していくなかで、2代目・専好の指導を受けるようになった。2代目は先代よりもさらに立体的な作風で知られた。その後5年間、2代目は凡下の立場で天皇に召し出されて宮中の立花御会の判者を務めた。

　現存する絵巻物（池坊専好立花図）には左右非対称に7本の枝が描かれているが、これは七つの山に囲まれた須弥山が示す仏教の世界観、三千世界を象徴している。その後、それほどフォーマルではなく、座敷に生ける投入というスタイルも生まれ、複雑な決まりに従わずに花の自然な美しさを表現できるため、町民に好まれた。

■envoy 使節　■hermitage 修道院、庵　■school 流派　■free-standing 支柱なしで立っている　■predecesor 前任者　■commoner status 一般庶民　■asymmetric 非対称の　■Buddhist cosmic idea of Sumeru 須弥山が示す仏教の世界観、三千世界　■townspeople（the 〜で）特定の町の町民

33 Yamada Nagamasa
Pioneer in Thailand

In about 1612, Yamada Nagamasa from Sunpu traveled to Siam on a merchant ship to trade overseas. Nagamasa settled in the Siamese capital that is now called Ayutthaya, and in **roughly** 1620, he became the leader of the Japanese community there known in Siamese as *Ban Yipun*, "Japanese village." He promoted trade and diplomatic relations between Siam and Japan. There was a market for deer **hide** in Japan, and in return he brought silver, swords, lacquer boxes, and high-quality paper back to Siam.

Nagamasa was granted a prestigious official title after he gathered a Japanese force and led it into battle **on behalf of** King Songtham during a successful struggle for power. When the king died and a **succession dispute** followed in 1628, Nagamasa led some 20,000 Siamese and 800 Japanese to secure the throne for the king's son. That however was the high point of his career.

As the political situation in Siam changed, he and 300 other Japanese were **banished** to a distant southern region by a rival of the royal family. In this remote location, he was wounded in battle by invaders and died from poison **administered** by his Siamese servant. Nagamasa's son then escaped to Cambodia.

Nagamasa was once **hailed** in Japan as a pioneer of Thai-Japanese cooperation and friendship, especially during Japan's imperialist period. But the **interpretation** of his activities is not so positive in Thailand. **Setting that aside**, he was deeply involved in trade between the two countries and in the politics of the kingdom of Siam. (253)

山田長政

日タイ関係を築いた先駆者

[?-1630]

　1612年頃、駿府（現・静岡）出身の山田長政は海外貿易を行うため、商船に乗ってシャム（タイの旧名）に渡った。現在アユタヤと呼ばれる首都に定住すると、1620年頃から、シャム語で「日本町」を意味する「バン・イープン」の首長となり、シャムと日本の貿易・外交関係を発展させた。日本には鹿皮の市場があり、代わりに日本からは銀や刀、漆塗りの箱、上質な和紙などをシャムに持ち帰った。

　長政は、ソンタム王のために日本人隊を集めて内戦・外征に参加して功を立て、最高の官位を授かる。1628年にソンタム王が亡くなり、**後継者争**いが勃発すると、長政は約2万人のシャム兵と800人の日本人兵を率いて、ソンタムの息子の親王を王位に就かせるが、このときがキャリアの頂点だった。

　シャムの政情が変化すると、長政は他の日本人300人とともに、王家の対立する勢力によって南方の僻地に**左遷**された。長政はこの辺境の地で侵略軍との戦いで負傷した揚げ句、シャム人の侍臣に毒を**盛ら**れて亡くなった。その後、長政の息子はカンボジアに逃れた。

　長政は、特に帝国主義時代の日本では、日本とタイの協力関係と親善を築いた先駆者として**評価**されていたが、タイでは（内政に干渉した外国人として）長政の活動はそれほど肯定的には**捉え**られていない。とはいえ、日タイ貿易やシャム王国の内政に深く関わっていたことは事実である。

■ roughly およそ　■ hide 皮　■ on behalf of 〜のために　■ succession dispute 家督争い　■ banish 追放する　■ administer（薬などを）投与する　■ hail 称賛する　■ interpretation 解釈　■ setting that aside その話は別として

34 Ihara Saikaku
Writer of the Floating World

Asai Ryoi's "Tales of the Floating World", *Ukiyo monogatari*, was the first well-known work to focus on a portion of Edo society where people **lived for the moment** and strived to **keep up with** the style of the times. But it was Ihara Saikaku who stands out as the representative of Genroku **prose** culture.

Son of a townsman, Saikaku had no interest in continuing the family business. Instead, he wandered the country, studied poetry, and achieved a reputation as a **virtuoso** in the popular poetry contests due to his wit. With his first prose work, however, he founded a completely new genre of fiction: tales of the floating world (*ukiyo zoshi*).

Combining an elegance of style and vocabulary with themes that appealed to the **emerging** townsmen of the cities, his "The Life of an Amorous Man" quickly became popular among readers. The work tells of a young man of **dissolute** habit who enjoys the pleasures of the beauties of the **pleasure quarters** before sailing off to an island inhabited solely by women, with irony and a comic tone.

The format of the publication was also important, for while he illustrated the first edition of the book himself, the woodblock print artist Moronobu illustrated the first edition that was published in Edo. In this case and others, **it is significant that** word and image were intimately related in Genroku culture and later culture as well. (234)

井原西鶴

浮世を描いた人気作家

［1642-1693］

　浅井了意の『浮世物語』は、江戸社会の一面に焦点を当て、浮世暮らしをしながら時代の流れに必死に合わせようとした庶民を描いた元祖的作品としてよく知られているが、元禄時代の散文文化を代表する存在といえば井原西鶴である。

　西鶴は町人の息子として生まれたものの、家業を継ぐ気はなく、諸国を遍歴して俳諧を学び、俳諧興行での才気煥発ぶりから一躍有名になる。そして最初に手掛けた散文（小説）作品で、それまでの小説ジャンルとは一線を画した「浮世草子」という形式を生み出した。

　当時、台頭した都市の町人たちを引き付けるテーマを流れるような文体と語彙で表現したこの『好色一代男』は、たちまち人気を集めた。同作品は、放蕩な若者が遊女たちと浮名を流し、やがて女性ばかりが住む女護島に船出する一代記を、皮肉を交じえて滑稽に描いている。

　出版の形式も重要で、最初の出版（大坂）では西鶴自らが挿絵を手掛けたが、江戸で出版された初版は浮世絵版画家の菱川師宣が挿絵を描いている。この作品以外でもそうだが、言葉とイメージが元禄文化とその後の文化に密接に関わった意義は大きい。

■live for the moment 刹那的に生きる　■keep up with ～に遅れずについていく
■prose 散文体　■virtuoso 名人　■emerging 新興の　■pleasure quarters 遊
郭　■dissolute 自堕落な　■it is significant that ～は重要である

35 Matsuo Basho
Traveling Haiku Master

When the poet Matsuo Basho moved to Edo, he joined the **lively debates** about different schools of poetry and took particular interest in linked-verse **competitions**, in which poems were connected in meaningful **progressions**. His poems became known for their **wordplay**, **earthy** humor, elegant **allusions**, and parodies of the classics.

Eventually he focused on three-line segments, of five, seven, and five **syllables**, making it into an independent poem known as *haikai* or *haiku*. Basho used this extremely short form to express **sentiments** of universal significance, describing daily scenes such as a frog jumping into a pond or a **cicada screeching** in the mountains.

Basho began a series of five journeys in 1684. Welcomed by local leaders, he spent evenings exchanging poems with his hosts. The most widely celebrated of his travels resulted in *Oku no hosomichi*, "The Narrow Road to the Deep North", describing his travels from Edo to Tohoku and down the coast of the Sea of Japan. Like other **travel diaries**, this work mentions places famous for their beauty, such as Nikko and Matsushima, as well as for their historical meaning, such as Hiraizumi where Yoshitsune met his tragic end. During this particular journey, he developed his poetic principle of *sabi*, a **synthesis** of gorgeous and lonely beauty. This work is **one of the high points** in the history of the Japanese poetic diary.

Basho's high **reputation** among contemporary and later poets **rests on** his **elevation** of haiku into a mature art form, his apparent union with nature, his humanism, and his appeal to poets of widely different **temperaments**. (261)

松尾芭蕉

俳句を芸術に高めた旅する俳人

[1644-1694]

　松尾芭蕉は江戸に出てくると、俳壇の活発な議論に参加し、特に意味のある句をつなげていく句合（左右の人が発句を作り優劣を競う）に関心を抱いた。芭蕉の句は、言葉遊び、俗っぽいユーモア、優雅な引喩、古典のパロディーなどで知られるようになった。

　芭蕉はやがて、五・七・五の音節を持つ3行の独立した句、いわゆる俳諧や俳句を重視するようになり、極めて短い形式で、蛙が池に飛び込む水音や山の中で鳴いている蝉の声といった日常的な情景を表現し、普遍的な情緒を表現した。

　芭蕉は1684年から5回にわたって旅に出ている。地元の有力者に迎えられた芭蕉は、夜になると宿の主人との間で句を交わした。そうした旅路の中でも最もよく知られているのが、江戸から東北、そして日本海沿岸を巡ったときのことを記した『奥の細道』である。同作品は、他の紀行と同様、日光や松島などの名所、源義経（p.42）が悲劇的な最期を遂げた平泉など、歴史的な意味を持つ場所にも触れている。この特別な旅で芭蕉は、豊かで閑寂な美が合わさった「寂」という自身の俳句の神髄を究めていった。『奥の細道』は、日本の歌人・俳人による日記の歴史において白眉に数えられている。

　芭蕉が同時代と後世の俳人の間で高く評価されているのは、俳句を成熟した芸術に昇華させ、その句にまざまざと自然との調和や人間性を表しているからで、そうした句に、さまざまな気質の俳人たちも引き付けられているのである。

■ lively debate 活発な議論　■ competition 競争、コンテスト　■ progression 連続　■ wordplay 言葉遊び　■ earthy 野卑な　■ allusion 引喩　■ syllable 音節　■ sentiment 感情　■ cicada 蝉　■ screech 鋭い声で鳴く　■ travel diary 旅日記　■ synthesis 統合　■ one of the high points 素晴らしいものの一つ　■ reputation 評判　■ rest on 〜に基づく　■ elevation 上昇　■ temperament 気質

36 Chikamatsu Monzaemon
Kabuki for Everyone

Kabuki **owed** a great deal **to** both *noh* and *kyogen*, the main forms of theater in the medieval era. However, it **incorporated** elements of dance, narrative storytelling, and costumes that attracted a much broader audience. During the Genroku era, a sophisticated form of Kabuki developed, with all roles played by men. The plays came from war tales (*gunki*), classic *noh* dramas, and puppet plays (*joruri*). Several **playwrights** and actors of superb ability transformed Kabuki into a stage art which **captivated** both the elite and the **commoners** alike.

It was the romanticist Chikamatsu Monzaemon who took theater performance to its full potential, by showing how the claims of duty or obligation (*giri*) and the pull of human feelings (*ninjo*) affected people of the Genroku era. He was particularly concerned with the lower-class townsmen.

Through his characters, Chikamatsu showed how hard it was for people of various classes to live **in accord with social conventions**, traditions, and morality. He pitted the individual against the social environment of his day. His historical plays (*jidaimono*) are derived from the same kinds of narrative materials that Japanese **chanters** used for centuries. When his Kabuki plays were staged as bunraku, puppet theater, Chikamatsu increased the excitement of the performance with supernatural feats that actors in Kabuki could not do.

Among his contemporary or domestic tragedies (*sewamono*), an actual double suicide of two **star-crossed** lovers in 1703 became the basis for his *Sonezaki Shinju*, which was first staged within a few months of the actual event. It quickly became a **staple** of both Kabuki and puppet theater. (260)

近松門左衛門

歌舞伎界のヒットメーカー

[1653-1724]

　歌舞伎は、中世の主要な演劇形態である能と狂言の両方の影響を大きく受けながら、舞いや物語性の高い語り、衣装といった要素を取り入れ、より幅広い観客を獲得した。元禄時代（1700年前後）には、洗練された歌舞伎の形式が生まれ、すべての役を男性が演じるようになる。演目の題材として下敷きにされていたのは、軍記や古典能、人形浄瑠璃などで、優れた劇作家や役者たちは歌舞伎を一つの舞台芸術に押し上げ、特権階級から庶民までもをとりこにした。

　義理と人情の板挟みを描いて芝居の可能性を最大限に引き出し、元禄時代の人々を魅了したのが、ロマン主義者の歌舞伎作者、近松門左衛門だ。近松が、特に関心を寄せたのは下層階級の町人だった。

　近松は作品の登場人物を通して、さまざまな階級の人々が社会の慣習や伝統、道徳にとらわれた生きづらさを描き、個人と当時の社会環境を対峙させた。近松の「時代物」（歴史上の出来事を基にした作品）は、何世紀にもわたって浄瑠璃の太夫らが用いてきたのと同じ語りの題材から生まれている。近松の歌舞伎の作品が浄瑠璃（文楽）として上演される際には、近松は生身の歌舞伎役者にはできそうにない非現実的で度肝を抜くような演出を盛り込んだ。

　当時の社会で起きた悲劇的な事件を主題にした「世話物」と呼ばれる作品ジャンルでは、近松は、1703年に実際に起きた薄幸な恋人同士の心中を下敷きにした『曽根崎心中』を事件から数カ月後に初演。同作品は、すぐに歌舞伎でも浄瑠璃でも定番の作品となった。

■ owe … to ～に…の借りがある　■ incorporate 取り入れる　■ playwright 劇作家　■ captivate 魅了する　■ commoner 庶民　■ in accord with ～に合わせて　■ social convention 社会慣習　■ chanter 詠唱者　■ star-crossed 薄幸な　■ staple 定番

37 Ichikawa Danjuro I
Evolution of Kabuki

The two most famous names in Kabuki during the Genroku period were Ichikawa Danjuro in Edo and Sakata Tojuro in Osaka. Danjuro was influenced by an early form of puppet theater that dealt with the **martial exploits** of a **semi-legendary** hero named Kimpira. In **portraying** Kimpira, Danjuro developed a style of acting that became known as *aragoto*, "rough business." It is a style that combines **exaggerated postures**, brightly colored costumes, and vivid makeup. He was so successful at this **swaggering** style and became so popular among theater goers that he was widely **imitated** by other Edo performers.

People who are not familiar with arts such as Kabuki may not realize that subsequent actors may succeed to an actor's name. Danjuro trained his own son, for example, and the son eventually took the name Danjuro II. The son was also **inventive** and became known for **premiering** the majority of the **celebrated works** known as *Kabuki juhachiban*. Danjuro VII formally established these works as the special **repertory** of the Ichikawa family.

Danjuro IX helped to elevate the status of Kabuki to a theater of respectability and contributed to the the stability of Kabuki as it experienced major social and cultural changes in the **chaotic** second half of the 19th century. This same Danjuro became the teacher of the founder of another, somewhat more progressive, family that took the name Ichikawa Ennosuke. (229)

市川団十郎（初代）

歌舞伎界の革命家

［1660-1704］

　元禄歌舞伎の2大巨頭として知られた江戸の市川団十郎と上方の坂田藤十郎。団十郎は、金平という伝説的な豪傑の武勇伝を題材にした初期の浄瑠璃「金平浄瑠璃」の影響を受け、金平を演じる際に、その後、荒事芸として知られるようになった誇張的な姿勢（六方）、色鮮やかな衣装、鮮やかな隈取を組み合わせた演技様式を確立。見得を得意とした団十郎は芝居好きの人々の間で人気を博し、江戸の歌舞伎界で次々に模倣者を生んだ。

　歌舞伎などの芸能に通じていないと、役者の名前が受け継がれることを知らないかもしれないが、団十郎の場合は息子を育成し、その息子が2代目・団十郎を襲名。2代目も創意工夫に富み、歌舞伎十八番（『助六』など）と呼ばれる著名な作品の大半を初演したことで知られている。7代目は、そうした作品を市川家の特別な演目として正式に確立した。

　9代目は、19世紀後半の混乱期に社会や文化が大きく揺れ動く中、歌舞伎の社会的地位の向上に尽力し、歌舞伎が不動の地位を築くのに貢献した。9代目の門弟は、その後、より新取の気性に富んだ名跡、市川猿之助の初代となった。

■martial 武芸の　　■exploit 偉業　　■semi-legendary 伝説的要素の多い
■portray 演じる　　■exaggerated 誇張された　　■posture 姿勢　　■swaggering
ふんぞり返った　　■imitate まねる　　■inventive 発明の才がある　　■premier 初演
する　　■celebrated work 有名作品　　■repertory レパートリー　　■chaotic 混沌
とした

38 Tokugawa Yoshimune
Shogunal Reformer

The eighth shogun of the Tokugawa shogunate, Tokugawa Yoshimune is known for using his practical experience as a daimyo to **maximize** his direct knowledge of shogunate affairs and administration.

His most novel method of gaining knowledge was the *meyasubako*, a box for "appeals" (*meyasu*). A suggestion box was placed outside one of the gates of Edo Castle in 1721 for the use of **peasants** and **townspeople**. The locked box was carried to the shogun, who personally read the comments, suggestions, and **complaints**. As a result of one suggestion from a physician, a hospital was established at Koishikawa. Another was the creation of a city-wide **fire-prevention** program.

Earlier shoguns had depended on personal attendants to carry out the administration, but Yoshimune made his own appointments and developed a **core** of officials who carried out a series of reforms known as the Kyoho Reforms.

These reforms restored the shogunate as a whole and the samurai as a class to financial **solvency**. It meant rejecting the **extravagant** lifestyle of earlier shoguns and making his own lifestyle more **spartan** and **frugal**. By doing this, he sought to improve the **morale** of the samurai class.

Persuaded by his advisers, Yoshimune lifted all restrictions on the importation of foreign books, in Chinese and Dutch, as long as they did not touch on the forbidden subject of Christianity. He **patronized** scholars of any school of thought whose ideas might be useful. He sponsored the study of Dutch language and Western learning because he hoped they would **be of practical value** to the shogunate. (257)

徳川吉宗

改革に励んだ将軍

[1684-1751]

　江戸幕府 8 代将軍・徳川吉宗は、藩主時代（紀伊、現・和歌山）の実務経験を基に、実践的な知識を幕政に**最大限**に生かしたことで知られている。

　民心を把握するために吉宗が導入した最も斬新な方法が「目安箱」だ。1721年、江戸城の門外に**百姓**や**町人**のための投書箱が設置された。施錠された箱は吉宗の元に運ばれ、吉宗自らが庶民の直訴や陳情、**苦情**などに直接目を通し、ある町医者からの提案を受け入れて小石川に養生所を設立したり、別の訴えからは江戸市中の**防火**制度を整えたりした。

　それまでの将軍は側用人に頼って行政を執行していたが、吉宗は自ら任命に関わり、**中核**となる幕臣の登用制度を整備し、享保の改革と呼ばれる一連の改革を行った。

　享保の改革によって吉宗は、幕府全体と武士階級を**財政的**に立て直し、それまでの将軍の**贅沢**な暮らしぶりを改め、自らも**質素倹約**に励み、武士階級の士気向上に努めた。

　側近らの説得を受け、信仰が禁じられていたキリスト教に関わりのないものに限り、漢訳洋書や蘭語書籍の禁輸制限を解除。有用と思われる思想であれば、どのような分野でも学者の**後ろ盾**となり、幕府に**実用的な価値**をもたらすと考えた蘭語や西洋の学問の研究を支援した。

■ maximize 最大限に活用する　■ peasant 農民　■ townspeople 町民
■ complaint 苦情　■ fire-prevention 防火　■ core 中心メンバー　■ solvency
資力　■ extravagant 浪費する　■ spartan 質素な　■ frugal つましい　■ morale
士気　■ patronize 支援する　■ be of practical value 実用的に価値がある

39 Motoori Norinaga
Capturing Japanese Origins

In the 18th century Japanese began to **be preoccupied with** what they considered their cultural uniqueness, focusing on the ancient past. National Learning (*kokugaku*) scholars, such as Kamo no Mabuchi and Motoori Norinaga, began rejecting the Neo-Confucian ideas from China that the Tokugawa government adopted. These scholars began studies of ancient Japanese sources, trying to find what had been done before the influence of China arrived.

To capture this spirit of Japan, these scholars focused first on poetry, especially the *Man'yoshu*. In this ancient poetry, they found a feeling for nature and an expression of emotion that **preceded** Chinese influence.

Motoori Norinaga **argued** that the moral teachings of Buddhism and Confucianism were **vain** and insincere. Those foreign traditions, he contended, were formalistic and **rigidly** logical. They denied the "pure Japanese heart (*yamatogokoro*)" that had been so beautifully expressed in the early works of literature before foreign influence appeared. He **claimed** that literary study of the *kokugaku* scholars aimed at what he called *mono no aware*, a sympathetic awareness of the sadness of things.

Norinaga's **seminal** work, *Kojiki-den*, provided a careful reexamination of the *Kojiki*, and it took him 35 years to complete. It is still an essential study of the *Kojiki* today. In later years, the studies of the *kokugaku* scholars were used as evidence supporting the mythology of the **divine descent** of the emperor and the central position of the imperial house within Japanese culture. But now, the works of Norinaga and others are key introductions to Japanese culture. (250)

本居宣長

日本の源流を探った国学者

［1730-1801］

　18世紀になると、日本人は自国の文化特有と思われるものに**関心を持ち**始め、古代に注目するようになった。そうした中で、賀茂真淵や本居宣長といった国学者は、徳川幕府が中国から取り入れた新儒教思想（朱子学）を否定するようになり、中国の影響が**及ぶ前**に日本でなされていたことを探るため、日本の古道研究を始めた。

　日本の精神を捉えるために、宣長らがまず注目したのが和歌、特に『万葉集』だった。この古代の和歌の中に、宣長らは中国の影響を受けるようになる前の日本にあった自然を愛でる情緒や感情表現を見いだした。

　宣長は、仏教や儒教の道徳的な教えは**無益**かつ偽善的であり、他国のそうした慣習は形式的で**堅苦しい**論理的な概念で、他国からの影響が発現する前の初期の文学作品に見事に表現されていた「純粋な日本人の心（大和魂、大和心）」を否定していると**主張**。国学者らの文学研究で目指したのは、日本文学が有していたしみじみとした哀愁を解する「もののあはれ」だと唱えた。

　宣長の**代表作**『古事記伝』は、『古事記』（古代天皇の伝承）を入念に考察し、35年をかけて完成させたもので、現在でも『古事記』研究には欠かせない作品となっている。後年、宣長ら国学者の研究は、日本文化における天孫降臨神話や皇室の中心的地位を裏付ける証拠として用いられていたが、現在は、宣長らの著作は日本文化を知る重要な入門書という位置付けにある。

■ be preoccupied with ～に夢中になる　■ precede ～よりも先に起こる　■ argue 主張する　■ vain 無益な　■ rigidly 厳格に　■ claim 主張する　■ seminal 画期的な　■ divine descent 神聖な血統

40 Honda Toshiaki
Far-sighted Surveyor

Born on the Japan Sea coast in the late Edo period, Honda Toshiaki was a mathematician, and a **political economist**. At the age of 18 he went to Edo in order to study mathematics and geography. There he opened his own academy and studied Dutch, the language of Western learning.

An accomplished navigator, he maintained close relations with northern explorers including Mamiya Rinzo, and in 1801 he captained a vessel that surveyed Ezo, now called Hokkaido.

Having seen the effects of the Tenmei **famine**, he **did his best to** determine how Japan might increase its wealth in order to overcome the pressure of people on the limited land area of Japan. Honda became convinced that Japan's economic problems could be solved by following European models, particularly that of England.

In *Keisei hisaku* (*A Secret Plan for Governing the Country*), he identified four top priorities for Japan's future: gunpowder, **precious metals**, shipping, and the colonizing of Hokkaido. The development of explosives could lead to the opening of channels for rivers and the mining of precious metals. Metals would not be exported but used to produce goods of greater value for trade abroad. He even proposed moving the capital from Edo to Kamchatka—because the latter was at the same latitude as London. His advice also included the **abandonment** of national seclusion (*sakoku*), a **state-managed** foreign trade, and overseas colonization.

Honda was wise enough not to publish his treatise. He thereby escaped the punishment that was the fate of Hayashi Shihei, who was arrested for criticizing official policies. (256)

本多利明

先見性を持った経世家

[1743-1820]

　江戸時代後期に日本海沿岸（越後、現・新潟）に生まれた本多利明は、和算家（数学者）、経世家としても知られている。18歳のときに江戸に出て算学と地理を学び、私塾を開き、西洋の学問である蘭学を学んだ。

　熟練した探検（調査）家として、間宮林蔵をはじめとする北方探検家と親交を深め、1801年には蝦夷地（現・北海道）の調査船を指揮した。

　天明の飢饉の影響を目の当たりにした利明は、狭い国土の人口増問題を打破するために国力を増強する方法を探るのに全力を尽くし、日本の経済問題は欧州、とくにイギリスのモデルに倣えば解決できるかもしれないと確信するようになった。

　自著『経世秘策』の中では、日本の今後の最優先課題として、火薬・貴金属・船舶の活用、蝦夷地開発などの4つを挙げている。火薬の開発は、河川水路の開削や鉱産資源の採掘につながる可能性がある。金属は、そのまま輸出してしまうのではなく、商品の製造に用いたほうが、貿易でより高い価値を生み出せる。利明は、カムチャッカの緯度がロンドンと同じであることから、江戸からカムチャッカへの遷都も提言。その他、開国（鎖国廃止）、幕府主導の交易、植民地政策なども唱えた。

　本多利明は賢明にも自身の論説を刊行しなかったため、同じく経世家で、幕政を批判した林子平のように蟄居を命じられることはなかった。

■political economist 政治経済学者　■famine 飢饉　■do one's best to 最善を尽くして〜する　■precious metals 貴金属　■abandonment 放棄　■state-managed 国営の

41 Ino Tadataka

Geographer par excellence

While working in his adoptive family's business, Ino Tadataka studied astronomy and **calendar making**. At the age of 49, he headed to Edo to study under the official astronomer of the Tokugawa shogunate, Takahashi Yoshitoki.

Armed with his master's knowledge of mathematics and science, in 1800 Ino **was commissioned by** the shogunate to conduct a geographic **exploration** of Hokkaido. He was the first to use Western scientific methods in his **surveys**. With this as a beginning, he went on to **survey** the entire country, making use of precision instruments for his **astronomical observations**. By the age of 70 he had covered over 40,000 kilometers surveying the country.

After his death, his friends and students completed his maps and in 1821 they compiled a collection of 225 maps of the entire country. Based on his actual surveys of Japan's coastlines and inland areas, these came to be known generally as "the Ino maps."

Yoshitoki's better-known son Kageyasu collected the maps and completed them in 1821. They are the first in Japan to include **longitude** and **latitude** and also list the detailed names of **domains, shogunal lands**, temples, shrines, towns, and villages. They also indicated accurate distances between points in a system that used the imperial capital of Kyoto as the base for his **prime meridian.**

Until the 1880s his maps were used as models for mapmaking. They were so accurate that many of them continued to be used by the Japanese army well into the twentieth century. They are also valued for their **aesthetic** quality in addition to their accuracy. (259)

伊能忠敬

前人未到の偉業を達成した地理学者

［1745-1818］

　伊能忠敬は養家の家業（酒造）に携わりながら、天文学と暦学を学んだ。49歳で江戸に渡り、幕府天文方の高橋至時に師事する。

　至時から数学と科学の知識を授かった伊能は、1800年に幕府から蝦夷地（現・北海道）沿岸の測量を任され、初めて西洋の科学的手法で調査を実施。これを皮切りに、精密機器を用いて全国を天文測量し、70歳になるまでに踏破した距離は4万キロ以上に及んだ。

　死後、弟子らが地図を完成させ、1821年に225図の日本全国を網羅した『大日本沿海輿地全図』を作成した。この地図は、忠敬が実際に測量した全国の海岸線や内陸部の地図を基にしたもので、一般的に「伊能図」と呼ばれるようになる。

　至時の著名な息子、高橋景保の監督下でまとめられ、1821年に完成を見たこの地図には、日本で初めて経線と緯線が記載されており、国郡や天領、寺社、町、村落などの名称も詳細に記されている。また、忠敬が（当時）本初子午線の基準とした京都改暦所を通る正確な子午線も示されている。

　1880年代まで、忠敬の地図は地図製作の際に原図として使用され、精度の高さから、20世紀に入ってからも多くの地図が日本軍に利用された。また、その精密さに加え、芸術性の高さも評価されている。

■calendar making 暦作り、暦学　　■be commissioned by 〜に委託される
■exploration 探査　■survey 測量（する）　■astronomical observation 天文測量　■longitude 経度　■latitude 緯度　■domain 領地　■shogunal land 幕府の領地　■prime meridian 本初子午線　■aesthetic 美的な

42 Tsutaya Juzaburo
Making Art and Writing Available

The innovative publisher Tsutaya Juzaburo established **a commanding presence** in Edo. In addition to **being acquainted with** a number of leading writers and intellectuals, he **is credited with** discovering new talent, particularly Utamaro.

Born in the Yoshiwara pleasure quarter, in the 1770s Juzaburo successfully introduced a new format for guidebooks to the beauties of Yoshiwara. Juzaburo opened a shop outside the quarter where he sold courtesan critiques and guidebooks, eventually **monopolizing** these guidebooks called *Yoshiwara saiken*. Publishers like Juzaburo contributed to the development of light fiction that **daringly satirized** officials and treated the world of Yoshiwara with only **transparent disguises**. New writers like Kyokutei Bakin and Santo Kyoden produced yomihon that exported the tastes, fashions, language, and outlook of Edo throughout Japan. At various times Juzaburo offered lodgings to Bakin, Kyoden, and Utamaro, who stayed with Juzaburo until the latter's death.

Juzaburo **was inventive in** incorporating wood-block prints into his publications. In the early 1790s, he published single-sheet *ukiyo-e* prints of beauties and actors, concentrated on illustrated books of poetry, and bought up **printing blocks** of illustrations from other publishers reissuing them under his own **imprint**.

The Tokugawa government frequently tried to **censor** books and prints, and Kyoden and Juzaburo were involved in a celebrated censorship case in 1791 as a result of the Kansei Reforms. Kyoden was punished for writing three "depraved books" (*sharebon*) and Juzaburo was **fined** half of his personal wealth for having published the them. But Juzaburo's contribution to publishing and **implementing** collaboration between writers and artists remain as a significant legacy. (256)

蔦屋重三郎

アートと書籍を身近に
［1750-1797］

　革新的な手法で知られた出版業者、蔦屋 重 三郎は、江戸で圧倒的な存在感を放っていた。当時の代表的な作家や知識人の多くと知り合いで、喜多川歌麿をはじめとする新しい才能を発掘したといわれている。

　遊郭があった吉原に生まれた重三郎は、1770年代に吉原の遊女を紹介する新形態の案内書「細見」を売り出して評判を得る。その後、吉原の外に店を開き、遊女評判記や吉原の案内書を販売し、「吉原細見」と呼ばれるようになったこうした書を一手に手掛けるようになった。重三郎ら、この時代の版元は、役人を大胆に風刺した戯作の発展に貢献し、吉原の世界をありのままに伝えた。曲亭馬琴や山東 京 伝といった新進作家は読本（伝奇小説）を通じて、江戸の嗜好や流行、言葉、考え方を全国に発信した。馬琴や京伝、歌麿らはさまざまな時期に重三郎の下に居候し、とくに歌麿は自身が亡くなるまで居候を続けた。

　重三郎は版画を出版物に取り入れることでも独創的な才能を示した。1790年代初頭には、美人画や役者絵の浮世絵を 1 枚刷りで出版し、絵入狂歌本に力を入れ、他の版元から版木を買い取って自身の版元に刷らせた。

　徳川幕府はたびたび書物や版画に発禁処分を下し、京伝と重三郎は寛政の改革によって1791年に摘発される。京伝は 3 冊の洒落本が禁令を犯したとして処罰を受け、重三郎はそれを出版したことで罰金として私財の半分を没収されたが、重三郎が出版業に貢献し、作家と絵師の合作に寄与した業績は重要な遺産である。

■commanding 堂々とした　■presence 存在感　■be acquainted with 〜と知り合いである　■be credited with 〜の功績があるとされる　■monopolize 独占する　■daringly 大胆に　■satirize 風刺する　■transparent 包み隠しのない　■disguise ごまかし　■be inventive in 〜に発明の才がある　■printing block 版木　■imprint 出版社　■censor 検閲する　■fine 罰金を科す　■implement 実施する

43 Daikokuya Kodayu
Starting with a Shipwreck

Kodayu was captain of the *Shinsho-Maru* when it was blown off course on its way to Edo. It ended up on Amchitka Island in the Aleutian Islands. At that time, the land was **sparsely** occupied by Russians and **Aleuts**. Eventually Kodayu and the Russians were able to return to Asia landing in eastern Russia.

Kodayu traveled to St. Petersburg, for an audience with Catherine the Great. He is sometimes considered to mark the beginning of Russian interest in Japan.

After staying in Russia to 1792, he returned to Japan with Adam Laxman. This Russian military officer was **dispatched by** Catherine the Great to collect information about Japan and to discuss establishing commercial relations between the two countries, using the occasion of returning a Japanese to his homeland. The Russian officials reached Nemuro and **proceeded** overland **to** Hakodate and Matsumae. They were met by a shogunate representative, who prevented them from going to the capital. The representative accepted Kodayu and his **cohorts**, formally exchanged gifts with the Russians, but refused to discuss the question of trade.

For his **violation** of the Tokugawa shogunate's policy of **national seclusion**, Kodayu was sentenced to **house arrest** for life in Edo and was closely interrogated about his experience in Russia and his knowledge of the outside world.

He made a major contribution to Japan's understanding of the outside world through reports **compiled by** shogunate scholars, including Katsuragawa Hoshu, a scholar of Western Learning. Hoshu's **chronicle** of the adventures of the **shipwrecked** seaman became *Hokusa bunryaku*, published in 1794. (253)

大黒屋光太夫

日露関係に影響を与えた漂流者

[1751-1828]

　神昌丸の船頭だった大黒屋光（幸）太夫は、江戸に向かう途中、嵐で遭難し、アリューシャン列島のアムチトカ島に漂着した。当時、島にはロシア人とアレウト族（先住民族）がわずかながら住んでいた。その後、光太夫はロシア人とともにロシア東部に上陸し、アジア大陸に戻ることができた。

　光太夫はサンクトペテルブルグ（首都）でエカチェリーナ2世に拝謁。これを機にロシアが日本に関心を抱くようになったという説もある。

　光太夫は1792年までロシアに滞在した後、ロシア軍将校、アダム・ラクスマンとともに帰国する。ラクスマンは、エカチェリーナ2世に命を受けて派遣されており、目的は光太夫を帰国させる機に乗じて日本についての情報を収集し、両国の通商関係を確立する協議に持ち込むことにあった。ロシアの使節団は根室に到着し、陸路で函館と松前に向かい、幕府の代表団に面会するが、江戸行きを阻止される。幕府の代表団は光太夫一行を受け入れ、ロシア側と正式に贈り物を交換したが、貿易についての協議は拒否した。

　光太夫は、幕府の鎖国政策に違反していたため、江戸の屋敷内に生涯留め置かれる処分を下され、ロシアでの経験や外界で得た見聞について厳しく尋問された。

　光太夫の体験は一方で、蘭学者の桂川甫周ら、幕府お抱えの学者がまとめた報告書を通じて、異国の理解に大きく貢献した。のちに甫周は遭難した漁師、光太夫による冒険年代記『北槎聞略』を1794年に刊行した。

■sparsely まばらに　■Aleut アレウト人　■be dispatched by 〜に派遣された
■proceeded to 〜に向かう　■cohort 仲間　■violation 違反　■national
seclusion 鎖国　■house arrest 自宅軟禁　■compiled by 〜に編纂された
■chronicle 年代記　■shipwrecked 難破した

44 Katsushika Hokusai
Never-Ending Print Artist

Katsushika Hokusai began his career in the studio of Katsukawa Shunsho, a specialist in portraying actors, **courtesans**, and sumo wrestlers. Hokusai was soon assigned a series of portraits of actors. His reputation spread and in 1791 the publisher Tsutaya Juzaburo invited him to design a few woodblock prints, the beginning of **a long association**. After Shunsho died, Hokusai began to **integrate** influences from the delicate classical Rimpa school, other Japanese influences, Chinese painting, and Western perspective. What resulted was a unique Hokusai style.

From 1796 onward, he created illustrations, commercial prints, books, and, under the name Hokusai, prints and paintings. Around 1800 he began referring to himself as *Gakyojin Hokusai*, "the man mad about painting," and **earned notoriety** for living as a **recluse**, painting obsessively and with boundless energy, developing a superb sense of design and proportion.

In cooperation with the artist Bokusen, he began producing *Hokusai manga* (Sketches by Hokusai), a series of picture books. His landscape print series *Fugaku sanjurokkei* (Thirty-Six Views of Mt. Fuji) began to appear by 1831 and through the following decade, he designed woodblock prints of subjects from waterfalls to birds to ghosts. In 1834 he produced his masterpiece illustrations *Fugaku Hyakkei*, One Hundred Views of Mt. Fuji.

More than any other Japanese works of art, Hokusai's "Great Wave off Kanagawa" and "Fuji in Clear Weather" are known around the world. A case of cross-cultural exchange, he **borrowed from** the West and contributed to the French Impressionists and other Western artists of the late nineteenth century, including Monet and Van Gogh. (257)

葛飾北斎

描くことに取りつかれた浮世絵師

［1760-1849］

　葛飾北斎は、役者絵、花魁などの美人絵、相撲絵などを専門としていた勝川 春 章の門下となり、すぐに役者絵を手掛けるようになった。評判が広まり、1791年に版元の蔦屋 重 三郎（p.94）に版画の下絵を数点依頼され、以来、長い付き合いとなった。春章の死後、北斎は繊細で古典的な琳派をはじめ、日本のさまざまな絵画の流派、中国画、西洋の遠近法などの影響を融合させるようになり、独自のスタイルとして結実させていく。

　1796年以降は、挿絵、商業版画、読本を手掛け、北斎の名で版画や絵を制作。1800年頃から「画 狂 人北斎」の画号を用いるようになり、世捨て人同然の暮らしぶりで世間の不評を買いながらも取りつかれるように絵に没頭し、飽くなきエネルギーで圧倒的なデザイン力とバランス感覚を身に付けていった。

　浮世絵師の牧墨僊の協力のもとにその後、『北斎漫画』の制作を開始。1831年頃から富士山を題材とした風景版画集『富嶽三十六景』を発表し、その後の10年間、滝、鳥、幽霊などを題材にした版画を制作。1834年には、傑作である『富嶽百景』を制作した。

　北斎の『神奈川沖浪裏』や『凱風快晴』は、日本絵画の中で世界的に最も有名な作品だ。北斎は異文化交流を地でいくように、西洋絵画の手法を取り入れる一方で、フランスの印象派をはじめ、モネやゴッホなど19世紀後半の西洋の芸術家たちにも影響を与えた。

■courtesan 高級娼婦　■a long association 長い付き合い　■integrate 統合する　■earn notoriety 不評を買う　■recluse 隠遁者　■borrow from 〜を借用する

45 Utagawa Hiroshige
Capturing Landscapes on Paper

Ando Tokutaro entered the studio of Utagawa Toyohiro, and was given the name Hiroshige and **the right to use** the Utagawa name. Among his first works were book illustrations and single-sheet prints of actors and beautiful women. Around 1830 he was invited by a publisher to design a set of ten views of the city of Edo. Combining **startling** designs and details, these novel wood-block prints made the locations both familiar and strikingly new.

Of the five national roads of the Edo period, the most traveled was the Tokaido connecting Edo and Kyoto. Hiroshige made the stations of that road famous around the world. In 1832 he traveled the road, a journey that **prompted** his best-known set of prints, Fifty-three Stations of the Tokaido Road (*Tokaido gojusantsugi*). It was the first of 20 sets he created.

Hiroshige also designed sets of ten views each for Kyoto and Osaka, and took over the completion of a set of seventy prints of the mountainous Nakasendo road from Edo to Kyoto. His well-known Thirty-six Views of Mt. Fuji (*Fuji sanjurokkei*) were published after his death.

Although Hiroshige painted other subjects, he was more of a specialist in landscapes than the dynamic Hokusai. In Hokusai's landscapes, the people and the setting are both important, but in Hiroshige's landscapes, the setting dominates and the atmosphere is created by the season, weather, time of day, and the perspective. His pictures are **reminders** of the **vastness of nature** and the **insignificance** of **human beings**. One finds dramatic seasonal and weather changes in his works, but they convey a basic tranquility. (263)

歌川広重

風景を紙に写し取った巨匠

[1797-1858]

　安藤徳太郎（幼名）は歌川豊広（浮世絵師）に入門し、広重の名を与え
られ、歌川を名乗ることを許される。初期には、挿絵や役者絵、美人絵と
いった1枚刷りの版画などを手掛けた。1830年頃、版元から江戸の名所10
カ所を集めた作品（『東都名所拾景』）を依頼される。斬新な構図とディテ
ールを組み合わせたこの木版画は、各地に親しみとはっとするほど新しい
視点を与えている。

　江戸時代の五街道のうち、最も通行量が多かったのは江戸と京都を結ぶ
東海道だった。その宿場は、広重の絵によって世界中に知られることとな
る。1832年、広重は東海道を旅し、それをきっかけに代表作となる浮世絵
版画集『東海道五十三次』を制作。20種類にわたる東海道シリーズの最
初の作品となる。

　広重は、それぞれ10枚ものの『京都名所』『浪花名所図絵』も手掛け、
江戸と京を結ぶ、峠の多い中山道を描いた70枚の連作を引き継いで完成さ
せた。有名な『冨二三十六景』は死後に刊行された。

　広重はさまざまな題材を描いているが、風景画に関してはダイナミック
な画風の北斎（p.98）よりも専門とした。北斎の風景画では人物と場所が
重きをなすが、広重の風景画ではその場所そのものが重要な要素で、季節
や天候、時間帯、遠近法によって情緒が醸し出されている。広重の絵は、
自然の広大さと人間の卑小さを思い起こさせる。作品には季節や天気の劇
的な変化が見て取れるが、常に静謐感が漂っている。

■the right to use 使用する権利　　■startling 驚くべき　　■prompt 誘発する
■reminder 思い出させるもの　　■vastness of nature 自然の広大さ
■insignificance 取るに足らないこと　　■human being 人間

46 Toshusai Sharaku
Mysterious Master Artist

A mysterious genius named Toshusai Sharaku, whose dates are un-known, has fascinated the world for two centuries. All that is known for sure is that he produced some 140 woodblock prints, primarily of Kabuki actors and a few of sumo wrestlers, during a period of less than a year in 1794, perhaps **spilling into** 1795. All of his works were published by Tsutaya Juzaburo. He was relatively **obscure** in his own day, but was discovered in the Meiji period by Westerners as **one of a kind**.

His contemporary Utamaro specialized in pictures of courtesans, but Sharaku was a master of the actors of the Kabuki theater. While Utamaro's prints are sophisticated and the colors and composition are precise, Sharaku's colors sometimes **clash**, and his placement of his subject matter seem less precise. But what might be seen as failings actually enhance his reputation. Sharaku's portraits are **bursting with** energy. The faces of the actors and their bodies are filled with dramatic emotion.

Sharaku tried to portray real people, not just stereotypes. As mentioned, little is known about him. One theory is that he stopped producing works so suddenly because actors were angry at being portrayed so **unflatteringly**. How-ever, this seems **inconceivable**, because few other artists ever captured the essence of Kabuki like Sharaku did. **If anything**, the actors he chose to draw must have appreciated his exciting, vivid appreciation of their dramatic skills. The influence of Sharaku was not on contemporary artists, but on collectors and writers of his own and later period who have been moved by the power of his works. (263)

東洲斎写楽

謎に満ちた天才絵師

［生没年不詳］

　東洲斎写楽という謎の天才は、生没年不詳だが、200年前から世界中を魅了してきた。確実に分かっているのは、1794年からおそらく1795年にかけた１年足らずで歌舞伎役者と相撲取りを題材に約140点の浮世絵を制作したことだけだ。全作品は版元の蔦屋 重三郎（p.94）が出版した。当時はあまり知られていなかったが、明治期になり、個性的な存在として西洋で一躍知られるようになる。

　同時代の喜多川歌麿は遊女を専門に描いたが、写楽は役者絵の名手だった。歌麿の浮世絵版画が洗練され、色彩も構図も精密であるのに対し、写楽の作品は時に色彩がぶつかり合い、被写体の配置もデフォルメしすぎているように見える。だが、欠点と思われがちなそうした特徴で写楽は名声を博した。写楽の役者絵はエネルギーにあふれ、役者の顔や体には迫力があり、エモーショナルだ。

　写楽は紋切り型ではなく、リアルな人物を描こうとした。本人についてはあまり分かっておらず、突然、絵を描かなくなったのは、役者たちがあまりにありのままに描かれることに腹を立てたせいではないかという説もある。だが、写楽ほど、歌舞伎の本質を捉えた浮世絵師は稀だったことから、この説は説得力に欠ける。むしろ、写楽のモデルに選ばれた役者たちは、自分の演技に心躍らせ、鮮やかに捉えてみせた写楽を高く評価していたに違いない。写楽の影響は、当時の他の絵師には及ばなかったが、同時代、そして後世の収集家や作家たちの心を、作品の持つ力で大きく動かした。

■ spill into ～に流れ込む　　■ obscure 無名の　　■ one of a kind 唯一無二の
■ clash 調和しない　■ burst with ～ではちきれる　■ unflatteringly へつらわずに
■ inconceivable 考えられない　　■ If anything どちらかと言えば

47 Jippensha Ikku
Writing for Entertainment

Literature dealing with the "floating world" of the pleasure quarters reached its highest level in the works of Saikaku, but another, lighter style of writing followed his. Social commentaries on the people of fashion in Edo, focused on what was considered **chic** (*sui*) and **savoir faire** (*tsu*) among the non-elite. Called *gesaku*, this type of popular fiction was characterized by a **flippant** attitude, **hilarious** exaggeration, and **tongue-in-cheek** humor. It is filled with wordplay, parody of earlier works, and gossip about life in fashionable circles. What is happening at the theater and the pleasure quarters is the main subject matter.

In the early nineteenth century, the most commercially successful author of this light fiction was Jippensha Ikku. **Renouncing** his samurai status, he began his career as a *bunraku* playwright in Osaka. He then moved to Edo and began to write prose literature, as the **protege** of the publisher Tsutaya Juzaburo. His most popular work is *Tokaidochu Hizakurige*, "A Journey by Foot." It is translated and published in English as *Shank's Mare*. This volume follows the adventures of two **light-hearted** characters as they pass along the Tokaido highway on foot from Edo to Kyoto and Osaka. If Saikaku is sophisticated, *Hizakurige* is **bawdy**, carefree, and completely entertaining. It shows a world that is entirely **secular**, **lusty**, and **irrepressible**.

Ikku was active in the field of the comic verse called *senryu* and was also an accomplished artist who illustrated many of his own works, including *Hizakurige*. According to his contemporary Kyokutei Bakin, Ikku was the first fiction writer in Japan able to earn a living **solely** from the **proceeds** of his books. (269)

十返舎一九

娯楽読み物の第一人者

［1765-1831］

　遊郭の「浮世」を扱った文学が最高潮に達したのは井原西鶴（p.78）の作品においてだが、その後、もっと軽妙な文体の作品も生まれた。江戸の時流に乗った人々について風刺し、庶民の美意識である「粋」や「通」を取り上げた「戯作」と呼ばれるこの大衆小説の特徴は、**軽妙洒脱**さ、**面白おかしい誇張表現**、**皮肉**が利いたユーモアだ。言葉遊びや過去作品のパロディー、社交界のゴシップなどが盛り込まれ、芝居小屋や遊郭の出来事が主な題材となっている。

　19世紀初頭、この戯作の分野で最も商業的に成功した作家が十返舎一九だ。一九は、武士の身分を**捨て**、大坂で文楽の作家として活躍し始める。その後、江戸に移り住み、版元の蔦屋重三郎（p.94）の**居候**となり、散文文学を書き始めた。最も人気を集めた代表作は『東海道中膝栗毛』。『Shank's Mare』として英語版も出版されている。江戸から京都、大坂までの東海道を歩くお気楽な主人公2人の道中記で、井原西鶴が洗練された作風とすれば、こちらは**みだら**で屈託がなく、とことん**愉快**な作品で、非常に**世俗的**で、**活力に満ちた**世界が描かれている。

　一九は、諧謔（ユーモア）を交えた短詩、川柳の分野でも活躍し、さらに優れた画家として『東海道中膝栗毛』をはじめとする多くの自著の挿絵を自ら手掛けた。同時代の戯作者、曲亭馬琴によれば、一九は日本で初めて**執筆料だけ**で生計を立てた職業作家だった。

■chic 粋な　■savoir faire 如才のなさ　■flippant 不真面目な　■hilarious 抱腹絶倒の　■tongue-in-cheek ふざけた、皮肉な　■renounce 捨てる　■protege 被保護者　■light-hearted 悩みのない　■bawdy 卑猥な　■secular 世俗の　■lusty 活力に満ちた　■irrepressible 快活な　■solely ～だけで　■proceeds 売り上げ

48 John Manjiro

From Fisherman to Government Interpreter

Fourteen-year-old Nakahama Manjiro was a young Tosa fisherman who **was shipwrecked** with others during a storm on the **deserted island** of Torishima south of Edo in 1841. An American **whaling ship** found them on the island and took them aboard and they joined the crew whaling in the north Pacific. The ship passed through Hawaii and his companions stayed there. But Manjiro was invited to go to the United States by the captain, who had been impressed by his intelligence. The captain gave him the name John Mung, which was easier for the crew to **pronounce**, although he later also used the name John Manjiro.

Arriving in New Bedford in 1843, he was taken in by the captain's family. After gaining basic education at school, he studied mathematics, **navigation**, **surveying**, **coopering**, and other useful skills. He returned to Japanese soil in 1851 and was **interrogated** by authorities in Satsuma and Nagasaki. Although the officials did not trust Manjiro completely, they realized that he had a lot of information about the West that could benefit them.

When Commodore Perry arrived in Japan in 1853, Manjiro was called into service as a translator. He was appointed to serve as an instructor at the Naval Training Center. He acted as the chief interpreter for the shogunate **embassy** that traveled to the United States to ratify the Harris Treaty of 1858. After the Meiji Restoration, he was appointed an instructor at the Kaisei Gakko, now Tokyo University. (242)

ジョン万次郎

漁師から幕府の通訳になった男

[1827?-1898]

　土佐（現・高知）の漁師だった中浜万次郎は、14歳だった1841年、仲間と漁に出ているときに嵐に巻き込まれ、江戸南方の無人島・鳥島に漂着。アメリカの捕鯨船に発見、救助され、北太平洋で捕鯨している乗組員に加わった。船がハワイに寄港した際、仲間はそのままハワイにとどまったが、その頭の良さに感心した船長にアメリカ行きを誘われる。万次郎は、他の乗組員が発音しやすいジョン・マンという愛称を船長につけてもらい、その後、ジョン万次郎という名も使用するようになった。

　1843年にニューベッドフォード（東海岸）に到着すると、船長の家族に迎え入れられ、学校で基礎教育を受け、数学、航海術、測量、造船など、有益な技術を学び、1851年に日本に帰国。薩摩藩と長崎奉行所の取り調べを受ける。役人たちは万次郎を完全に信用したわけではなかったが、万次郎が西洋に関するさまざまな情報を持っており、そうした情報が自分たちにとって役に立つことを認識するようになった。

　1853年にペリー提督が来航した際には、万次郎は幕府に召聘されて通弁（通訳）を務め、軍艦操練所教授方に任命された。1858年の日米修好通商条約批准のために幕府の使節団が渡米した際にも通弁主務を務め、明治維新後は開成学校（東京大学の前身）の教授に就任した。

■ be shipwrecked 難破する　■ deserted island 無人島　■ whaling ship 捕鯨船
■ pronounce 発音する　■ navigation 航海術　■ surveying 測量学　■ cooper
たる（状のもの）を作る　■ interrogate 尋問する　■ embassy 外交使節団

49 Yoshida Shoin
Patriot Idealist

During the Bakumatsu period, Japan was divided between pro-shogunate and anti-shogunate camps. **Further** complicating political affairs was how to **deal with** the **imperialist** intentions of the Western nations. Among those who took an active part in these confrontations was Yoshida Shoin, a teacher, writer, and **proponent** of *sonno joi*, "**revere** the emperor and **expel** the barbarian."

Influenced by the teachings of Yamaga Soko on military sciences and loyalty to the emperor, Yoshida Shoin attempted to **stow away on** the flagship of Commodore Perry, the USS Powhatan. His purpose was supposedly to learn about the West in order to strengthen Japan. It was a unique aim, for a scholar of Confucianism, to insist that Japan should acquire Western learning and technology.

Caught before the ship departed, he was imprisoned and later placed **under house arrest**. In his house, he established the *Shoka Sonjuku*, an academy where he taught young samurai including Ito Hirobumi and Yamagata Aritomo, who would later play key roles in the Meiji Restoration. They were attracted to his intense idealism and his belief that practical action and setting a personal example were immensely important.

His passionate patriotism involved him in an unsuccessful attempt at **assassinating** the high shogunal official Manabe Akikatsu. He was arrested, tried, and executed in 1859 during the Ansei Purge. As an anti-shogunate activist seeking to **undermine** the power of the government, he became a **martyr** and a model for those ready to take action in support of their social and political views. (248)

吉田松陰

愛国心に燃えた理想主義者

[1830-1859]

　幕末の日本は佐幕派と倒幕派に二分されていた。さらに政情を複雑化していたのが、欧米列強の帝国主義的な外圧にいかに対処するかという問題だった。こうした論争に積極的に関わったのが吉田松陰（長州藩士）だ。松陰は教育者でも著作家でもあり、尊王攘夷（天皇尊崇と外国人排斥）派だった。

　松陰は、山鹿素行が唱えた山鹿流の兵法と尊王論に影響を受け、ペリー提督の旗艦、ポーハタン号で密航を企てた。国力増強のために西洋について学ぶためだったとみられている。日本は西洋の学問と技術を習得すべきだという主張は、儒教学者としては特異なものだった。

　出航前に捕まった松陰は投獄され、その後、国許蟄居処分を受ける。ここで「松下村塾」を主宰し、後に明治維新の中心となる伊藤博文や山県有朋ら、若い志士たちを指導する。博文らは、松陰の強烈な理想主義と、実践的な行動、自ら模範を示すことこそが非常に重要だと説く信念に引き付けられた。

　愛国心に燃えていた松陰は、幕府老中・間部詮勝の暗殺を企てるが失敗し、捕えられ、評定所で取り調べを受けて、1859年の安政の大獄で刑死した。幕府の権力を打倒しようと倒幕派として活動した松陰は、社会的・政治的見解のために行動を起こすことも辞さない人々にとっては殉教者であり、模範というべき存在となった。

■further さらに　　■deal with 〜に対処する　　■imperialist 帝国主義的な
■proponent 支持者　■revere 崇める　■expel 追放する　■stow away on
（船）にこっそり乗り込む　■under house arrest 自宅に軟禁されて　■assassinate
暗殺する　■undermine 損なう　■martyr 殉教者

50 Sakamoto Ryoma
Determined Activist

Prior to the Meiji Restoration, action, commitment, and **extremism** replaced the **conformity** of Tokugawa rule. During this period, Sakamoto Ryoma from Tosa domain became a pro-emperor anti-foreign activist.

During the Ansei Purge in 1858, Sakamoto became deeply involved in national politics. He fled Tosa, took up the life of a masterless samurai, and in 1862 plotted to assassinate the high-ranking shogunate official and modernizer Katsu Kaishu. When Sakamoto confronted Katsu, however, **the latter** convinced Sakamoto to listen to his ideas first. In the end, Katsu persuaded Sakamoto about the need for building up national strength before trying to expel the foreigners and Sakamoto became Katsu's follower.

Sakamoto promoted naval and shipping training, set up trading operations in Nagasaki, and imported arms for anti-shogunate domains. When the shogunate **took a hard line against** pro-imperial loyalists, he sought protection in Satsuma, the **epicenter** of the anti-shogunate movement. He became a major figure in the establishment of an alliance between Satsuma and Choshu that led to Choshu's victory over the Tokugawa army.

Sakamoto's wide contacts and his pro-imperial ideas became attractive to his former superiors in Tosa, who hoped for a **negotiated settlement** with the Tokugawa. He became a national figure in the effort to force the resignation of the last Tokugawa shogun, leading to the restoration of the emperor to power.

He was assassinated in 1867 by a member of a pro-shogunate group of ronin. His correspondence and activities, however, reveal Ryoma to be an energetic, adaptable, determined, and optimistic figure, prepared to work for national unity and strength. (257)

坂本龍馬

決断力を備えた転換期の活動家

［1835-1867］

　明治維新以前、徳川幕府の**統治**に反旗を翻し、大義に身を捧げ、時に**急進主義**に走る藩士らも出てきた。この時期、土佐藩の坂本龍馬は尊王攘夷の志を持つようになる。

　龍馬は1859年の安政の大獄の頃に国政にのめり込むようになる。その後龍馬は脱藩し、1862年、近代化を推進していた幕臣、勝海舟の暗殺を企てる（諸説あり）。だが、いざ対峙した海舟に、まず自分の考えを聴くよう説き伏せられ、その結果、龍馬は外国人を排斥する前に国力を高める必要があると説得されて、勝の門下になった。

　龍馬は海軍操練所の設立を推進し、長崎で貿易会社を設立。輸入された武器を倒幕派の藩に**斡旋**した。幕府が尊王派に**強硬路線を取る**と、龍馬は倒幕運動の**中心**となっていた薩摩藩に庇護を求め、その後、薩長同盟成立の立役者となる。この同盟により、長州藩は幕府の長州征討を返り討ちにした。

　脱藩していた龍馬の幅広い人脈と勤王思想に興味を示したのは、徳川幕府と**交渉**して事態の**収拾**を図ろうとしていた土佐藩の上層部だった。龍馬は、徳川最後の将軍を大政奉還（政権を朝廷に返上する）させるために尽力し、名を馳せる。

　龍馬は1867年、佐幕派の浪人とみられる男に暗殺された。だが、残された書簡やさまざまな活動を見ると、龍馬はエネルギッシュで、順応性と決断力を備えた楽観的な人物で、日本の統一と国力増強のために働く覚悟をしていたことが分かる。

■ extremism 過激主義　　■ conformity 服従　　■ the latter（二者のうち）後者
■ take a hard line against ～に対して強硬政策を取る　　■ epicenter 中心点
■ negotiated settlement 交渉による和解

Chapter 3

近代・現代

Modern Period／Contemporary Period

Fukuzawa Yukichi

Saigo Takamori

Koizumi Yakumo

Shibusawa Eiichi

Emperor Meiji

Kitasato Shibasaburo

Kano Jigoro

Nitobe Inazo

Tsuda Umeko

Suzuki Daisetz

Minakata Kumagusu

Ogata Sadako

Natsume Soseki

Noguchi Hideyo

Tezuka Osamu

51 Saigo Takamori
Traditional Values and Courage

Satsuma samurai Saigo Takamori commanded the army that overthrew the Tokugawa shogunate and was a leader in the establishment of the Meiji government, which restored **sovereignty** to the Emperor in 1868. When the Iwakura Mission departed for the West in 1871, Saigo was left behind **in control of** the **caretaker** government. While the mission was abroad, the new government contemplated a **punitive expedition** against Korea. But when the Iwakura **entourage** returned with a broader experience of Western nations and realized what Japan needed to do before beginning any foreign adventures, the Korean adventure was set aside.

Saigo subsequently quit the national government and returned to Satsuma. Other unhappy samurai eventually persuaded him to lead a revolt against the new government in Tokyo. Saigo was dismayed by the action of these rebellious **disaffected** warriors, but resigned himself to take their side and lead an army to Tokyo to challenge the government. Yamagata Aritomo, architect of the modern Japanese army, led the government forces against this rebellion. It took the new government's forces six months to defeat the Saigo forces, **mobilizing** 65,000 men from its own police force and recruiting former samurai from other former domains.

The Satsuma Rebellion on 1877 ended in defeat for the rebels and Saigo **committed suicide**. The rebellion was the final major military challenge to the centralization of the Meiji government. Although he ended his life as a rebel, his popularity soared, because many saw him as a protester against **arbitrary** government, while others admired him as a **paragon** of traditional virtues, courage, and sincerity. (258)

西郷隆盛

伝統的な美徳を体現

［1827-1877］

　薩摩（現・鹿児島）藩士の西郷隆盛は、倒幕軍を指揮し、1868年の大政奉還による明治政府の樹立を主導した。1871年、岩倉使節団が欧米に出発すると、西郷は留守政府の統括を任された。使節団が海外にいる間、新政府は朝鮮出兵を検討する。しかし、岩倉使節団は欧米諸国で見聞を広めて帰国し、日本が海外で打って出る前にするべきことがあると考え、朝鮮出兵は中止された。

　西郷はその後、下野し、帰郷。そこで、東京の新政府に不満を持つ士族らに政府に対して蜂起するよう説得される。西郷は、こうした反逆的な不平士族たちの行動に落胆したものの、そちら側に付くことを受け入れ、反乱軍を主導（1877年に挙兵）。この反乱を鎮圧するために政府軍を率いたのが、日本軍の近代化を推し進めた山県有朋だった。新政府軍は西郷軍を撃退するまでに半年あまりを要し、警視隊や旧藩士ら約6万5,000人を動員した。

　西南戦争は西郷軍の敗北に終わり、西郷は自刃。この反乱は、明治政府の中央集権化に対する最後の大きな武装蜂起となった。西郷は反逆者として生涯を終えたが、専制的な政府に抗議したと多くの人に見なされ、その人気は高まり、さらには日本の伝統的な美徳や勇気、誠実さを体現した鑑としても賞賛された。

■ sovereignty 主権　■ in control of ～の主導権を握って　■ caretaker 暫定的な
■ punitive expedition 討伐　■ entourage 随行団　■ disaffected 反逆心のある
■ mobilize 結集する　■ commit suicide 自殺する　■ arbitrary 独裁的な
■ paragon 模範

52 Fukuzawa Yukichi
Explaining the West

Fukuzawa Yukichi is well known for actively introducing Western liberal ideas to Japan. In *Conditions in the West* (*Seiyo jijo*), based on his travels to the United States and Europe, he explained Western customs in **readily understandable** language. When the first section of this volume appeared in 1866, just before the Meiji Restoration, it sold an **estimated** 150,000 copies. In addition to the original publication, huge numbers of **pirated versions** went on sale.

Fukuzawa's work provided precisely the information that Japanese needed in order to understand the everyday **social institutions** of Western countries. He included sections on schools, taxation, newspapers, and hospitals.

In his *Encouragement of Learning* (*Gakumon no susume*) in 1876, he promoted the belief that everyone is **equal at birth** and that the main differences between people come from access to educational opportunities. In *An Outline of a Theory of Civilization* (*Bunmeiron no gairyaku*) and other works, he called for civil rights, the creation of a national **legislature**, and an increase in rights for women. In **preaching** the necessity of individual responsibility, he **urged** people **to** develop "the spirit of civilization" rather than simply aiming for producing and possessing material goods.

In addition to spreading these ideas through publications, he did the same through the establishment of what is now Keio Gijuku University. And although he chose not to be personally involved in politics, through the newspaper he **founded**, *Jiji Shimpo*, he constantly wrote editorials regarding virtually every aspect of public life in Japan. (246)

福沢諭吉

日本に西洋の思想や制度を紹介

［1834-1901］

　福沢諭吉は、西洋の自由主義思想を日本に積極的に紹介したことでよく知られている。自らの渡欧経験を基に記した『西洋事情』では、西洋の慣習などを分かりやすく説明。明治維新直前の1866年に刊行された初編の売り上げ部数は約15万部で、海賊版（偽版）も大量に出回った。

　福沢の著作は、欧米諸国で日常に利用される社会制度を日本人に理解させるのに必要な情報を的確に伝え、学校、税制、新聞、病院などの項目を立てている。

　1876年に完結した『学問のすゝめ』では、人は皆、生まれながらにして平等であり、他者との違いを生んでいるのは主に教育を受ける機会の有無との考えを唱えた。『文明論之概略』をはじめとする著作では、市民権、国会の開設、女性の権利拡大を訴えた。さらに、個人の責任の必要性を説き、世の人々に、物を作って所有することだけを目的にせず、「文明の精神」を養うよう呼び掛けた。

　福沢はこうした思想を著作を通じて説く以外に、現在の慶應義塾大学の設立などによって普及に努めた。自ら政治の世界に関わることはなかったが、自身で創刊した新聞『時事新報』では、日本の市民生活のほぼあらゆる面に関する問題を論説で取り上げ続けた。

■ readily たやすく　　■ understandable 理解できる　　■ estimated 推定で　　■ pirated version 海賊版　■ social institution 社会制度　■ equal 平等な　■ at birth 生まれたときに　■ legislature 議会　■ preach 説得する　■ urge … to …に〜するよう促す　■ found 設立する

53 Okuma Shigenobu
Iconoclast and Modernizer

In 1868, Okuma Shigenobu from Saga was appointed commercial official for the new government in Yokohama. Due to his financial **expertise** and **personal connections**, he was called to Tokyo, where after a few years he became minister of finance in 1873. As an "outsider" in the Satsuma-Choshu group that dominated politics, he was viewed with **a degree of suspicion**. Without the domainal political support that they had, he was forced to create alliances with various people. When he took a stand against a proposal to sell government assets to a **consortium** of businessmen who were from the Satsuma groups, he **was forced out of office**.

However, he remained active in politics, forming Japan's second major political party. In 1882, he also established Tokyo Senmon Gakko, which became present-day Waseda University.

Returning to politics in 1896, he served as foreign minister, then minister of agriculture and commerce. Forming the first party cabinet in Japan in 1898, with Itagaki Taisuke, he served **concurrently** as foreign minister and prime minister. Resigning in 1907, he became president of Waseda University. He was appointed prime minister again in 1914 and served two years before retiring permanently.

As a **proponent** of modernization and an **iconoclast**, he constantly fought against the one-sided use of power by the Satsuma and Choshu factions. He instead sought popular support, believing that all men, not just the elite of several former domains, **were entitled to** participate in the governing of Japan. In this respect, he was a **forerunner** of the democracy that developed in Japan's post-World War II era. (258)

大隈重信

因習を打破した近代化の推進者

［1838-1922］

　1868年、佐賀出身の大隈重信は維新政府に登用され、横浜で外国事務局判事を務める。その後金融知識と**人脈**を買われて東京に招聘され、数年後の1873年には大蔵卿（現・財務大臣）に就任。しかし、政界を牛耳っていた薩長閥からは「部外者」として**不信の目**を向けられ、旧藩の政治的支援を得られないなか、さまざまな人々と協力関係を築くことを余儀なくされた。薩摩出身の実業家らの関西貿易商会に官有物を払い下げようとする提案に反対したことで**政府を追われた**。

　しかし、その後も政界で活躍し、日本第2の主要政党（立憲改進党。のちに進歩党）を結成。1882年には早稲田大学の前身となる東京専門学校を設立した。

　1896年に政府に復帰し、外務大臣、農商務大臣を歴任。1898年に板垣退助とともに（自由党と進歩党を合同して憲政党を結成し）日本初の政党内閣を組み、外務大臣と首相を兼務した。1907年に辞任し、早稲田大学総長に就任。1914年に再び首相に就任し、2年後に退任した。

　近代化を提唱し、**因習打破**に努めた大隈は、薩長閥に偏った権力行使に抵抗し続ける一方で、藩出身のエリート層だけでなく、すべての人が日本の政治に参加する**権利**があると考え、国民に支持を求めた。こうした点で大隈は、第2次世界大戦後の日本で発展していく民主主義（女子教育や議会主義など）を体現する**先駆者**であった。

■expertise 専門知識　■personal connections 人脈　■a degree of suspicion 疑惑の程度　■consortium 企業連合　■be forced out of office 職を追われる　■concurrently 同時に　■proponent 支持者　■iconoclast 因習打破主義者　■be entitled to 〜する資格がある　■forerunner 先駆者

54 Shibusawa Eiichi
The Original Businessman

Shibusawa Eiichi played a prominent role in establishing industry in modern Japan. He **abandoned** his responsibility to succeed to his father's position as family head. Instead he went to Edo to **involve himself in** national politics.

As a **retainer** of a half-brother of the shogun, accompanying a government **entourage** to the International Exposition in Paris in 1867, he visited **dockyards**, factories, mills, iron foundries, banks, and social events. He realized that the source of wealth and power of any country **lay in** its economic and technological development. In Europe he realized several things. First, European businessmen enjoyed favorable social status and respect, unlike Japan's merchants (*shonin*). Second, Europeans owned and operated their own **enterprises** in cooperation with others. Third, stock exchanges and banks worked to support business.

Returning to Japan, he served in the Finance Ministry, where he led efforts to reform taxes and **survey natural resources**. He also played a key role in establishing the government-operated Tomioka silk-reeling mill. Entering the business world, he worked with others to form the First National Bank of Japan, where he educated bankers.

He helped organize several hundred industrial and commercial enterprises, from the manufacture of paper and cement to the operation of railways and insurance companies. He **coined** the new term *jitsugyoka*, a Japanese term for businessman. He helped form Japan's first Chamber of Commerce and contributed significantly to the country's first commercial high school, which later became Hitotsubashi University. As a **philanthropist** he promoted the national good and promoted the **ethics** of honesty, cooperative spirit, and **social responsibility**. (257)

渋沢栄一

日本の発展を築いた元祖実業家

［1840-1931］

　渋沢栄一は、近代日本の産業の発展に重要な役割を果たした。長男として父の家業（農業）を継がず、江戸に出て国政に関わるようになった。

　1867年のパリ万国博覧会の際は、将軍の異母弟の家臣として幕府の随行団に同行して渡欧し、造船所や工場、製作場、鋳物工場、銀行、社交行事などを視察。国の財力と権力の源は経済と技術の発展にあることを実感し、欧州でいくつかの点に着目する。それは第一に、欧州の実業家は、日本の商人とは異なり、社会的地位と尊敬を集めていること。第二に、欧州人は、他者と協力しながら自ら企業を所有し、経営していること。第三に、証券取引所や銀行がビジネスを支援していることだった。

　（明治維新後）帰国した渋沢は、大蔵省に出仕し、税制改革や天然資源の調査なども主導。また、官営の富岡製糸場の設立でも重要な役割を果たした。（退官後）財界に入ってからは出資者の協力を得ながら第一国立銀行を設立して銀行家の育成に携わった。

　製紙・セメント製造から鉄道・保険会社まで、数百社の工業・商社の組織化に尽力した。実業家という言葉を生み出したのも渋沢だとされている。日本初の商工会議所（の前身）や、同じく国内初の商業学校（一橋大学の前身）の設立に多大な貢献をした。慈善家としても国益を推進し、誠実さ、協調、社会的責任の倫理を説いた。

■ abandon 放棄する　■ involve oneself in 〜に関わる　■ retainer 家臣
■ entourage 随行団　■ dockyard 造船所　■ lay in 〜にある　■ enterprise 企業
■ survey natural resources 天然資源の調査　■ coin（新語を）作る
■ philanthropist 慈善家　■ ethics（複数形で）倫理　■ social responsibility 社会的責任

55 Tanaka Shozo
Pioneer environmentalist

A reformer who supported **peasants**, Tanaka Shozo **campaigned against political oppression** and industrial pollution. He was a leader in the local branch of the Freedom and People's Rights Movement (*Jiyu Minken Undo*), a nationwide political movement aimed at reforming the government along Western democratic lines.

He first entered the National Diet in 1890, where he fought against the pollution in the Kanto Plain by the Ashio copper mine. The mine company **dumped** large quantities of rock containing waste copper into the Watarasegawa and the Tonegawa rivers. Contaminated water flowed across farmlands downstream, poisoning crops and **affecting** thousands of farming families.

Tanaka stood for two principles. First, he believed that agriculture was the basis of the nation's livelihood and was more important than industry. Second, the livelihood and health of citizens should not be sacrificed for **public works projects** and industrial progress. **Disgusted at** the lack of attention to pollution-control regulations, Tanaka resigned his Diet seat.

In 1903 the government announced a plan to create a **reservoir** to control floodwaters that would mean the destruction of the farming community of Yanaka. Tanaka moved to Yanaka and led the villagers' protest against the government. They failed and their village **was razed**.

During his residence in Yanaka, Tanaka became a fellow worker, learning from farmers about quiet endurance and a lifestyle of **simplicity**. He made efforts to convey the need for human beings to respect the natural environment for their own survival. His long career of protest, rooted in traditional agricultural values, received little attention in his own day. Today, however, he is seen as an early **proponent of environmentalism**. (267)

田中正造

環境保護運動家の先駆け

［1841-1913］

　田中 正 造は、**政治的圧力にめげず、産業汚染に反対する運動を展開し、農民を支援**、欧米の民主主義に倣って政府の改革を目指した全国的な政治運動「自由民権運動」の地方支部で指導者を務めた。

　1890年に初めて国会議員となり、被害が関東平野に広がった足尾銅山の鉱毒汚染と闘った。足尾銅山を経営していた鉱業会社によって、銅の製錬による廃棄物を含んだ鉱石くずが大量に渡良瀬川や利根川に流れ込み、汚染水は下流の農地に流れ込んで作物を汚染し、多数の農家に**被害を与えて**いた。

　田中は二つの原則を大切にしていた。第一に、農業は国民の生活の基盤であり、工業よりも重要である。第二に、国民の生活と健康が**公共事業**や産業の発展を優先することで**犠牲**にされてはならないというものだ。公害の防止規制への関心の低さに憤慨した田中は議員を辞職した。

　1903年、政府は治水対策として**貯水池**建設計画を発表。それは、谷中という農村の廃村を意味した。田中は谷中村に移り住み、村人たちを率いて政府に抗議したが、訴えは通らず、村は**破壊された**。

　谷中村で暮らす間、田中は村民の仲間として働き、農民らから耐え忍ぶことと**質素な生活**様式を学び、人間が生存するには自然環境を尊重する必要があることを伝えていく取り組みを行った。田中は、伝統的な農業の価値観に根ざした抗議活動を長期にわたって続けたものの、当時は注目を集めることはほとんどなかった。だが今日では、**環境運動家の先駆け**と見なされている。

■ peasant 小作農　■ campaign against 〜に反対して運動する　■ political oppression 政治弾圧　■ dump 投棄する　■ affect 影響する　■ public works projects 公共事業　■ disgusted at 〜にうんざりして　■ reservoir 貯水池　■ be razed 破壊される　■ simplicity 質素　■ proponent of 〜の支持者　■ environmentalism 環境保護主義

56 Koizumi Yakumo

Taking Japan Outside

Successively abandoned by his Irish father, Greek mother, and his Irish great-aunt, Lafcadio Hearn was shipped off to America where he ended up in Cincinnati, Ohio. He found work with a local newspaper, becoming known for sensational accounts of local murders and **sensitive** accounts of the disadvantaged people of the city.

Establishing a **reputation** as a journalist, he moved to New Orleans, where he was fascinated by the city's distinctive Creole culture. His writings for national publications helped create the popular reputation of New Orleans. Growing **disenchanted with** the city, he then spent two years in the French West Indies.

In 1890 he travelled to Japan with a commission as a newspaper correspondent. The job was **terminated**, but he found a teaching position in Matsue, married Koizumi Setsu, the daughter of a samurai family, and became a Japanese citizen named Koizumi Yakumo. He was appointed to teach English literature at the University of Tokyo, a position he held until 1903. He continued to publish books about Japan's unique culture, a continuation of his fascination with exotic New Orleans and West Indies. When Japanese **aesthetics** became fashionable in the West due to the 1900 Paris Exposition, his writings became known around the world.

Some critics accused him of **exoticizing** Japan, but because he offered the West some of its first descriptions of Meiji period Japan, his work is valuable as a historical record of a culture no one else wrote about. Among his best works are a collection of lectures entitled *Japan: An Attempt at Interpretation* and *Kwaidan*, both published in 1904. (261)

小泉八雲

日本を海外に広く紹介

［1850-1904］

　アイルランド人の父、ギリシャ人の母、そしてアイルランド人の大叔母など親族にあまり恵まれなかったラフカディオ・ハーンはアメリカに渡り、オハイオ州シンシナティにたどり着き、新聞社に就職。地元で起きた殺人事件をセンセーショナルに報じる一方で、市内の恵まれない人々を繊細に描写して存在を知られるようになった。

　記者としての評判を確立した後、ルイジアナ州ニューオーリンズに移り住み、独特で多様なクレオール文化の魅力に引き込まれていく。ハーンによる全国紙の記事は、ニューオーリンズ人気を呼ぶことにもなった。だがハーンは、次第にこの街に幻滅し、フランス領西インド諸島で2年を過ごした。

　1890年に出版社の通信員として来日。この仕事は終了したが、島根県松江で英語教師となり、藩士の娘、小泉セツと結婚。日本に帰化し、小泉八雲を名乗った。東京帝国大学で英文学講師となり、1903年に退職。日本独自の文化や、なおも興味を抱いていた異国情緒あふれるニューオーリンズと西インド諸島を題材にした本を出版し続けた。1900年のパリ万博で日本の美意識が欧米で興味を持たれてブームになると、ハーンの著作は一躍、世界的に有名になった。

　ハーンの描く日本はエキゾチック（異国趣味）すぎるという批判もあるが、明治時代の日本を初めて西洋に紹介したという意味では、ハーンの作品は、（当時まだ）他に誰も書いていなかった文化的資料として貴重であった。代表作には、日本に関する講義集『日本――一つの解明』と『怪談』（いずれも1904年刊行）がある。

■ sensitive 繊細な　■ reputation 評判　■ disenchanted with ～に幻滅した
■ terminate 終わらせる　■ aesthetics 美学　■ exoticize エキゾチックに見せる

57 Emperor Meiji
Modern Transformer

Mutsuhito succeeded his father as emperor (*tenno*) in February 1867 and in 1868 his reign **was designated as** Meiji, "enlightened rule." The Meiji Restoration of 1868—formally on January 3, 1868—returned supreme authority for the administration of the country to the emperor. It established him as the **holder of sovereign power**, ultimate leader of the country's **armed forces**, and the center of **national morality**. The Shinto ceremonies **worked out** for his succession emphasized that the emperor stood at the point of unity between the present world and the unseen world of the gods.

During his long reign, Japan **transitioned from** a **feudal** agrarian country **to** a rapidly industrializing power. Government officials acting in his name possessed the real power, but he was a strong-willed person who exerted considerable personal power.

It is not easy to determine how much government policy came from "direct imperial rule" by Emperor Meiji acting as an individual. He endorsed the 1875 **edict** promising the establishment of a constitutional government, but on the whole, placing the emperor in a position somewhat above politics, maintaining the pose of a **benevolent father figure**.

He opposed copying the West and refused to set aside traditional rites and ceremonies. In addition, he exhibited an interest in maintaining historically important sites.

As the ultimate leader of Japan's armed forces during the Sino-Japanese War and the Russo-Japanese War, he monitored the situation closely. Some people think that stress during these periods left him exhausted. The death of Emperor Meiji symbolically brought an end to the era of Japan's successful **transformation into** a modern nation state. (265)

明治天皇

日本の近代化を体現

［1852-1912］

　睦仁親王は1867年に父を継いで天皇に即位。1868年に年号は明治と改元される。明治維新による王政復古で、国政の最高権力は天皇に復されてゆく。これにより、天皇が国の統治者と軍の最高指導者となり、国民道徳の中心となった。皇位を継承するために行われた神道の祭祀は、天皇が現世と目に見えない神々の世界をつなぐ立場にいることを強調するものだった。

　長い在位中、日本は封建的な農業国家から急速に工業国へと変貌を遂げていった。実権を握っていたのは天皇の名を借りて政治的決定を行う官僚ではあったが、明治天皇は剛毅な人物で、個人としての権威もかなり発揮した。

　明治政府の政策が、明治天皇の「親政」によってどの程度生み出されていたのかは判断し難い。明治天皇は1875年に立憲政体の詔書を発して立憲政府を樹立する一方で、概して政体よりやや超越した立場で、慈父のように臨み続けた。

　明治天皇は西洋を模倣することに反対し、伝統的な儀式や祭祀にこだわり、（皇室に関わりのある）歴史的に重要な史跡の保存にも関心を示した。

　日清戦争や日露戦争では大本営で軍を統帥し、戦局を注視。この時期のストレスで疲弊したという説もある。明治天皇の崩御は象徴的に、日本が近代国家への転向に成功した時代の終わりを意味した。

■ be designated as ～と呼称される　■ holder of sovereign power 主権者
■ armed forces 軍　■ national morality 国民道徳　■ work out 実施する
■ transitione from … to ～ …から～に移行する　■ feudal 封建的な　■ edict 勅
令　■ benevolent 慈悲深い　■ father figure 父親像　■ transformation into ～
への転向

58 Nagasawa Kanaye
Westernized Wine-maker

Originally from Satsuma domain in southern Kyushu, Isonaga Hikosuke, who took the name Nagasawa Kanaye, illustrates the drastic Westernization of a former samurai. At the age of fourteen, he and fourteen other young samurai left Satsuma **setting sail for** London in 1865, breaking the government's prohibition against foreign travel.

Their mission was to learn whatever they could about Western science and technology in order to help turn Japan into a modern society. Nagasawa first attended school in Aberdeen, Scotland, living with the family of Thomas Glover, a Scottish merchant, before going to London to study. There he met Thomas Lake Harris, who paid for his education in exchange for working at a **utopian colony** he was establishing in America.

Harris was the **spiritualist** founder of the **Brotherhood** of the New Life in New York State. Some 20 Japanese, including Mori Arinori, entered the brotherhood, although most eventually returned to Japan. Nagasawa stayed in America, served as Harris's secretary and rose to prominence within the brotherhood.

Harris moved the community to California in 1875 with a group of selected followers, including Nagasawa. They established a **wine-making venture** on a 2,000-acre **parcel** of land near Santa Rosa. Nagasawa later inherited the estate as sole owner. He maintained the community's wine-making business, Fountaingrove Winery, and became locally known as the "Wine King" of California. He was the first to introduce California wine to England and Europe, and to promote wine by inviting guests including Henry Ford, Thomas Edison, and Nitobe Inazo to the winery. (251)

長澤鼎

カリフォルニアでワイナリーを経営

［1852-1934］

　九州南部の薩摩藩出身の磯永彦輔は、のちに長澤鼎という変名を名乗った。長澤は、元武士が劇的な西洋化を遂げた様子を体現している。1865年、14歳のときに（藩命により）幕府の海外渡航禁止令を破って14人の若い藩士らとともに薩摩から船でロンドンに渡った。

　藩士らの使命は、西洋の科学技術についてできる限りのことを学び、日本（薩摩）の近代化に生かすことだった。長澤は、スコットランド、アバディーンで貿易商人トーマス・グラバーの家に下宿し、地元の学校に通った後、ロンドンで学んだ。そこでトーマス・レイク・ハリスと出会う。ハリスは、アメリカで理想郷のようなコロニー（共同体）の設立を目指しており、そこで働くことと引き換えに長澤の教育費を出すことを申し出た。

　ハリスは、ニューヨーク州で宗教共同体「新生兄弟会」を創設した神秘主義者だった。森有礼（長澤とともに渡米）を含む20人ほどの日本人が新生兄弟会に参加するが、大半は帰国。しかし長澤はアメリカにとどまり、ハリスの秘書のような役割を果たし、教団内で注目されるようになった。

　ハリスは1875年、長澤を含め、選りすぐりの信者らを連れてコミュニティーをカリフォルニアに移し、サンタローザ近郊の約800ヘクタールの土地にワイナリーを開設する。長澤はのち（ハリス死後）に、その農園を一人で引き継ぐ。教団の始めたワイン製造事業、ファウンテングローブ・ワイナリーを続け、地元でカリフォルニアの「ワイン王」として名を馳せるようになった。カリフォルニアワインをいち早くイングランドや欧州に紹介。ヘンリー・フォード、トーマス・エジソン、新渡戸稲造（p.136）らをワイナリーに招いてワインの普及に努めた。

■set sail for ～に向かって船出する　■utopian 理想郷の　■colony 共同体
■spiritualist 降霊術者　■brotherhood 協会　■wine-making ワイン造り
■venture ベンチャー事業　■parcel 一区画の土地

59 Kitasato Shibasaburo
Bacteriological Cures

Kitasato began studying medicine in his native Kumamoto Prefecture under the Dutch physician C.G. Mansvelt, then entered the Faculty of Medicine at the University of Tokyo. After receiving his M.D. degree in 1883, he carried out **bacteriologial** research at the government's Central Sanitary Bureau.

Kitasato went to Berlin to join the laboratory of bacteriologist Robert Koch. With Emil von Behring, he studied **tetanus** and diphtheria, two serious bacterial infections. In 1889 he succeeded in obtaining the world's first pure culture of tetanus bacteria. The following year, he and von Behring showed that **immunity** to tetanus could be achieved by an injection of **serum** containing an antitoxin. Opening a new field of science, they provided the first evidence that immune serum can serve in treating infections.

When he returned to Japan, with the assistance of Fukuzawa Yukichi, he established the Institute for Infectious Diseases in 1892. Two years later, the Japanese government sent him to Hong Kong during an epidemic of **bubonic plague**. He identified the *bacillus pestis* that causes the plague. The French bacteriologist Alexandre Yersin independently discovered the *bacillus pestis* in the same place and at the same time, and in the West, Yersin is **credited as** the discoverer.

With the assistance of colleagues, he established the Kitasato Institute in 1915. Kitasato later became the first dean of the Faculty of Medicine at Keio University and the first president of the Japan Medical Association. As a **physician** and bacteriologist, Kitasato's research and development of treatments for several **common** diseases contributed enormously to the health of people around the world. (260)

北里柴三郎

細菌感染症の治療法を確立
［1853-1931］

　北里柴三郎は故郷の熊本県でオランダ人医師C・G・マンスフェルトの下で医学を学び、東京医学校（現・東京大学医学部）に入学。1883年に医学博士の学位号を取得した後、内務省衛生局で**細菌学**の研究に従事した。

　その後北里はドイツのベルリンに渡り、細菌学者ロベルト・コッホの研究室に入る。エミール・フォン・ベーリングとともに**破傷風**とジフテリアという二つの重い細菌感染症を研究し、1889年、世界で初めて破傷風菌の純粋培養に成功。翌年、北里とフォン・ベーリングは、抗毒素を含んだ**血清**を注射することで破傷風の**免疫**が得られることを明らかにして、免疫血清が感染症の治療に役立つことを初めて証明、科学の新分野を切り開いた。

　北里は帰国後、1892年に福沢諭吉（p.116）の協力で伝染病研究所を設立した。その2年後、官命により、**腺**ペストが流行していた香港に派遣され、病原菌であるペスト菌を発見した。フランスの細菌学者アレクサンドル・イェルサンも、同時期に同じ場所でペスト菌を独自に発見したことから、欧米ではイェルサンが発見者とされている。

　1915年には同僚の協力を得て北里研究所を設立。その後、慶應義塾大学部医学科（現・慶應義塾大学医学部）初代医学科長、大日本医師会（現・日本医師会）の初代会長に就任する。**医師**で細菌学者だった北里の研究と、**公衆**の病気の治療法の進歩は、世界中の人々の健康に多大な貢献を果たした。

■ bacteriological 細菌学の　■ tetanus 破傷風　■ diphtheria ジフテリア
■ immunity 免疫　■ serum 血清　■ bubonic plague 腺ペスト　■ be credited
as ～として知られている　■ physician 内科医　■ common 一般的な

60 Kano Jigoro
From Judo to the Olympics

Kano Jigoro as an educator served as president of what became Tsukuba University. He believed strongly in the value of education which **comprised** improving knowledge, fostering **moral awareness**, and training the body.

Kano Jigoro, who stood a mere 157 cm (5 feet 2 inches) tall and weighed only 41 kg (90 lb), was bullied at school and took up jujutsu as a way of defending himself. He mastered classical jujutsu, **forged** new methods and techniques of training, and eventually renamed his complete fighting system "Judo." Kano founded the Kodokan in 1882 with less than a dozen students, but by 1911 there a thousand members enrolled.

Kano believed that physical education not only served to strengthen the physique, but also enhanced morality and consideration for others. Its ultimate aim was to achieve "maximum efficiency with minimum effort," to **perfect the self**, and make a contribution to society. **Winning at all costs** was not the goal.

In 1909 Japan received an invitation to participate on the International Olympic Committee (IOC). Kano was chosen as Japan's representative, the first representative from Asia. It was arranged that Japan would participate for the first time in the 5th Olympic Games held in Stockholm in 1912.

In part through his efforts, the 12th Olympic Games were scheduled for Tokyo in 1940. After the IOC meeting that made the decision, however, he died on his return voyage to Japan. Actually, it was not until the 18th Olympics that Japan was able to host its first Olympic Games and Judo became an official sport in the Olympic program. (259)

嘉納治五郎

五輪の日本開催に尽力した柔道家

［1860-1938］

　教育者として現在の筑波大学の前身（東京高等師範学校）の校長を務めた嘉納治五郎は、知識の向上、**徳義の涵養**、肉体の鍛錬から**成る**教育の価値を重視した。

　身長157センチ、体重41キロしかなかった嘉納は、学校でいじめられていたが、身を守るために柔術を習い始めた。古典的な柔術を習得した嘉納は、新しい訓練法と技を**確立し**、最終的に、自身が完成させた武術を「柔道」と名付けた。1882年に講道館を設立。10人ほどの学生が参加したが、1911年には在籍者は1,000人ほどとなる。

　一方で嘉納は、体育は体を鍛えるだけでなく、道徳心や思いやりの気持ちを強めるのにも役立つと考えた。最終的な目標は、「最小限の力で最大の効果を得る」ことで己を**完成させ**、社会に貢献することであり、**何が何でも勝つこと**を目標にしたわけではなかった。

　1909年、日本は国際オリンピック委員会（IOC）に招待され、嘉納はアジア初となるIOC委員に就任。1912年にスウェーデンのストックホルムで開催された第5回オリンピック大会に日本は初参加することとなった。

　嘉納の努力もあって、1940年には第12回オリンピック大会が東京で開催されることになった。IOC総会で東京大会が決定した後、嘉納は帰国する船上で死去した。結局、この大会は（戦争により）幻に終わり、日本がオリンピックを初開催し、柔道が正式種目になったのは、1964年の第18回大会である。

■ comprise 含む　■ moral awareness 道徳認識　■ forge 構築する　■ perfect the self 自己を完成させる　■ win at all costs どんなことをしても勝つ

61 Okakura Tenshin
Tea and the Arts

Okakura Tenshin, pen-name of Okakura Kakuzo, entered the newly created University of Tokyo and studied under Ernest Fenollosa, who promoted a **reassessment** of Japanese art and played a prominent role in efforts to preserve Japan's artistic treasures. Fenollosa worked ceaselessly to convince Japanese that their art was worth preserving and exhibiting. Because Japanese had little interest in native art works, Fenollosa purchased them at low prices, acquiring an outstanding private collection. Beginning as Fenollosa's student, Okakura eventually became a dynamic **colleague**.

After graduation, Okakura worked in the Ministry of Education and was sent to study Western art and art education in the West. When he returned, he and Fenollosa became founders of the official art academy, *Tokyo Bijutsu Gakko*, today's Tokyo University of Fine Arts and Music. Okakura also became a **curator** at what became today's Tokyo National Museum.

Resigning from the Ministry of Education, he lectured in America and Europe as a continuation of his efforts to educate the West about Asian, particularly Japanese, art. In 1903 he published *The Ideals of the East* and three years later published *The Book of Tea*. This latter work, originally published in English, gained him **recognition** abroad. It was the first introduction to the complex world of the tea ceremony, which in many ways **epitomizes** Japanese artistic culture.

He later became assistant curator to the Chinese and Japanese Department of the Boston Museum of Fine Arts, one of the finest collections of Japanese art in the world, including Fenollosa's private collection. (249)

岡倉天心

茶道と日本美術を欧米に紹介
［1862-1913］

　本名を覚三（かくぞう）といった岡倉天心（おかくらてんしん）は、新設された東京大学に入学後、日本美術の**再評価**を推し進めて日本の美術品の保存に多大な役割を果たしたアーネスト・フェノロサに師事した。フェノロサは、日本の美術品には保存・展示する価値があることを国民に訴え続けた。当時の日本人は国産の美術品への関心が薄かったため、フェノロサは日本の美術品を安価で購入し、傑出した個人コレクションを築いていった。最初（大学時代）はフェノロサの教え子だった岡倉は、その後、**同僚**として精力的に活躍するようになる。

　卒業後は文部省（現・文部科学省）に入り、西洋美術と美術教育を学ぶために欧米に派遣された。帰国してからはフェノロサとともに、官立の美術学校、東京美術学校（現・東京芸術大学）を設立。さらに、現在の東京国立博物館の**学芸員**（美術部長）にも任命された。

　文部省を辞めてからは欧米で講演するなど、アジアや特に日本の美術を欧米に紹介する取り組みを続けた。1903年に『東洋の理想』、その3年後に『茶の本』を出版。『茶の本』は、日本の芸術的な文化が**凝縮された**茶道の複雑な世界についての初の入門書というべきもので、もともとは英語で書かれていた。これにより、岡倉は海外で**知られる**存在となった。

　岡倉はその後、ボストン美術館の中国・日本美術部に迎え入れられた。同美術館は、フェノロサの個人コレクションを含む世界有数の日本美術コレクションを誇っている。

■reassessment 再評価　■colleague 同僚　■curator 学芸員　■recognition 認知度　■epitomize 縮図的に示す

62 Nitobe Inazo
Defining Bushido

The **term** *bushido*, which means "way of the warrior," became known to the West through the writings of scholar and educator Nitobe Inazo. Nitobe studied in the United States and Germany from 1884 to 1891 and received a **doctorate** from Halle University.

He was often asked by Westerners about moral education and religion in Japan. They found it hard to understand how Japanese were taught about **morality** when the school system established no formal syterm of religious teaching. Nitobe explained that there was a body of ethical teachings that had been taught to the warrior, *bushi*, class during the Tokugawa period. These teachings included justice, courage, **benevolence**, politeness, **honor**, and loyalty. Nitobe **contended** that these virtues had not disappeared after the Meiji Restoration. **To the contrary**, he claimed, these teachings had been adopted as ideals by all Japanese.

Nitobe published an explanation of these ideals in English in 1899 under the title *Bushido: The Soul of Japan*. This volume was influential around the world. U.S. President Theodore Roosevelt even recommended it as full of **insights** into understanding Japan. Published between Japan's victories in wars against China and then Russia, the world took this book as an explanation for why Japan had succeeded in becoming a powerful nation and began to consider *bushido* as a key concept in Japanese culture.

In addition to **stints** teaching at what is now Hokkaido University and the University of Tokyo, he served as **under-secretary-general** of the **League of Nations** and became chairman of the Japan Council of the Institute of Pacific Relations. (257)

新渡戸稲造

武士道を定義し世界に広める

［1862-1933］

　「武士道」という言葉は、学者（農政学）で教育者でもあった新渡戸稲造<ruby>に<rt></rt></ruby>の著作によって西洋に知られるようになった。新渡戸は1884年から1891年までアメリカとドイツに留学し、ドイツのハレ大学で**博士号**を取得している。

　新渡戸が西洋人からよく受けた質問は、日本の道徳教育や宗教に関することだった。日本人は学校で正式に宗教的な教育を受けていないにもかかわらず、どうやって**道徳**を学んでいるのか。新渡戸は、徳川時代の武士は、倫理的な教えとして、義、勇、仁、礼、**名誉**、忠義などを教わっていたと説明し、こうした価値観は明治維新後も廃れなかったどころか、国民道徳の柱として捉えられていると**主張**した。

　新渡戸は1899年にこうした日本人の心髄を英語で説明した『武士道』と題する本を発表。同書は世界中に影響を与え、アメリカのセオドア・ルーズベルト大統領も、当時、日本を理解する**ヒント**が詰まっているとして一読を勧めた。日本が日清戦争、日露戦争に勝利する間に出版されたこの本は、日本が強国として成功した理由を説明していると世界中に受け止められ、武士道は日本文化の重要な概念だと見なされるようになった。

　新渡戸は、現在の北海道大学、東京大学で教壇に立ち、**国際連盟事務局次長**、太平洋問題調査会の理事長などを歴任した。

■term 専門用語　■doctorate 博士号　■morality 道徳　■benevolence 仁愛
■honor 名誉　■contend 主張する　■to the contrary それと反対に　■insight
洞察力　■stint 一定期間の任務　■under-secretary-general 事務次長
■League of Nations 国際連盟

63 Mori Ogai
Broad-ranging Genius

Born Mori Rintaro, Ogai studied Confucian classics and Dutch, the language of Western medical studies in Japan. Moving to Tokyo, he took private lessons in German, which replaced Dutch in medicine and was admitted to the government medical school, now Tokyo University Medical School.

Upon graduation, he became a medical officer in the army, specializing in administration and hygiene. In 1884 he was sent to Germany for hygiene research. During those four years, he also read extensively in European literature. Returning to Japan, he campaigned for the development of scientific medical research, eventually becoming **Surgeon General** of the army.

Separate from the **pragmatic** world of medicine, he pursued a career as a writer. He published three short stories, including "The Dancing Girl" (*Maihime*) which reflected his experiences in Europe. Between 1892 and 1909 he focused on translations of European writers. When he resumed writing novels, however, he energetically published works based on his own experiences.

Stunned by the suicide of General Nogi Maresuke following the death of Emperor Meiji in 1912, he turned to historical stories and biographies of doctors of Chinese medicine in the late Edo period, including *Shibue Chusai* and *Izawa Ranken*, which Ogai considered two of his masterpieces.

Ogai's success as a writer comes from his ability to portray a **historical milieu** from his **self-proclaimed** status as a "bystander," who observes life as history in the making. Significantly, **in his will** he **stipulated** that on his tombstone he wanted no reference to his high rank in the army or other achievements. He wanted just his name inscribed: Mori Rintaro. (262)

森鷗外

多方面で活躍した天才
[1862-1922]

　本名は森林太郎という森鷗外は、漢学と、日本で西洋医学の言語として採用されていたオランダ語を学んだ。（出身地の現・島根県の石見国から）上京してからは医学に関してオランダ語に代わってドイツ語の個人指導を受けるようになり、官立の医学校（現・東京大学医学部）に入学した。

　卒業後は陸軍の軍医となり、治療と衛生を専門とする。1884年、衛生学を研究するためにドイツに派遣され、その4年間で鷗外は欧州の文学を多読した。帰国後は科学的な医学研究の発展に尽力し、その後、陸軍の軍医総監となる。

　鷗外は、**実用的な**医学の世界とは別に、作家としてのキャリアも追求し、欧州での経験を反映した『舞姫』など3編の短編小説を発表した。1892年から1909年にかけては欧州の作家の翻訳にも力を入れたが、小説の執筆を再開すると、自身の体験を下敷きにした作品を精力的に発表した。

　1912年、明治天皇（p.126）が崩御した後、乃木希典が殉死したことに**衝撃を受けた**鷗外は、歴史小説や幕末の漢方医の史伝を手掛けるようになり、そうした中で生まれた『渋江抽斎』『伊沢蘭軒』を自身の代表作と見なしていた。

　鷗外の作家としての成功は、**自ら**「傍観者」**と呼んだ**立場で人生を**歴史の流れ**として捉えたことにある。意義深いことに、鷗外は**遺書**で、自分の墓石には軍隊での高い地位やその他の業績を入れないよう**望んだ**。墓石に刻むよう望んだのは、森林太郎という名前、ただそれだけであった。

■Surgeon General 軍医総監　■pragmatic 実際的な　■stunned by ～に呆然として　■historical milieu 歴史状況　■self-proclaimed 自称の　■in one's will 遺言で　■stipulate 要求する

64 Tsuda Umeko
Educational Pioneer

Born the daughter of an expert on Western **agricultural** techniques, Tsuda Umeko was one of the first Japanese women to study overseas. She was only six years old when she became one of a group of students who were sent to the United States with the Iwakura Mission in 1871.

After she returned to Japan in 1882, she became a tutor in the **household** of the prominent Ito Hirobumi. She later taught at a new school for daughters of the **nobility**, Kazoku Jogakko. From 1889 to 1892 she studied a second time in the United States, at Bryn Mawr College.

In 1900 she founded the Women's English School (*Joshi eigaku juku*), which later became Tsuda College. She also served as the first president of the Japanese branch of the Young Women's Christian Association (YWCA).

Although the Education Order of 1872 established that boys and girls were to receive **primary education**, post-primary education for women was seriously limited. While public education at the secondary level through college was concentrated on males, schools for girls and women were private and often related to Christian missionary activities. At the time that Tsuda founded her school, most girls' high schools were privately operated and there was heavy demand for such institutions. In these circumstances, it was private educators like Tsuda who founded post-secondary institutions for women that offered **first-rate** academic studies. (227)

津田梅子

女子教育のパイオニア
[1864-1929]

　西洋農法の専門家の娘として生まれた津田梅子は、日本人女性として初めて海外留学した一人である。1871年、わずか6歳で留学生に選ばれ、岩倉使節団に随行して渡米した。

　1882年に帰国後、伊藤博文の家で住み込みで家庭教師として働き、その後、華族の子女向けの新しい学校「華族女学校」で教壇に立ち、1889年から1892年まで、アメリカに再度留学し、ブリンマー大学で学んだ。

　1900年には女子英学塾（津田塾大学の前身）を創立。キリスト教女子青年会（YWCA）日本支部の初代会長も務めた。

　1872年の学制では、男女共に初等教育を受けさせることが定められていたが、女子の中等・高等教育は大幅に制限されていた。男子は大学で公立の高等教育を受けられたのに対し、女子の場合はキリスト教の布教活動に関連した私立の学校であることが多かった。津田が女子英学塾を創立した当時、女子のための高等教育の場の大半は私塾的なものだったため、そうした機関への需要は非常に大きかった。こうした背景で、女子に一流の学問を提供する高等教育機関を設立したのが、津田ら私立学校の教育者たちだった。

■ agricultural 農業に関する　　■ household 家庭　　■ nobility 貴族階級
■ primary education 初等教育　　■ first-rate 一流の

65 Suzuki Daisetz

Zen Underpinnings of Culture

Known as Daisetz Teitaro Suzuki in the West, through his publications not only in Japanese but also in English, this philosopher played a major role in spreading the popularity of Zen Buddhism around the world.

While he was a student at the University of Tokyo, he **simultaneously underwent** Zen training in Kamakura. He trained under Shaku Soen, the **abbot** at Engakuji. In 1897 he moved to Illinois in the Midwestern U.S. to assist a publisher there with the English translation of Eastern philosophical and religious works. When he returned to Japan in 1909, he **was appointed to** teaching positions in English at Gakushuin Univerity, which was then known as the Peers' School. He married Beatrice Lane and until her death in 1939, she remained his close **collaborator** in his writings.

In 1921 he began teaching the philosophy of Buddhism at Otani University, in Kyoto. During the years that followed, he published a significant number of books. A three-volume series of essays that he published on Zen titled *Essays in Zen Buddhism* was the first major Western-language explanation of Zen Buddhism. Among his other important works, *Zen Buddhism and Its Influence on Japanese Culture*, published in 1938, had a major impact on the English-speaking world. It deepened Western understanding of many different aspects of Japanese culture, extending beyond the subject of religion into art and social attitudes. (226)

鈴木大拙

禅の世界的伝道者

［1870-1966］

　鈴木大拙は、欧米では鈴木貞太郎大拙の名で知られた哲学者で、日本語以外に英語でも出版された著作を通じ、禅思想を世界中に知らしめる上で大きな役割を果たした。

　帝国大学（現・東京大学）在学中に鎌倉で禅の修行を行い、円覚寺の管長、釈宗演の下で参禅。1897年、アメリカ中西部のイリノイ州に渡り、東洋哲学や宗教に関する書籍の英訳を手掛けていた出版社に編集員として勤めた。1909年に帰国後に、学習院教授に就任し、英語を教える。妻となったベアトリス・レーンは、1939年に亡くなるまで、鈴木の著作に協力し続けた。

　鈴木は1921年、京都の真宗大谷大学（現・大谷大学）で仏教哲学を教え始めた。その後、多数の書籍を出版。『禅論文集 1 - 3 』は、欧米の言語による禅についての初の本格的な解説書だった。重要な著作の中でも1938年に出版された『禅と日本文化』は、英語圏に大きな影響を与え、テーマが宗教のみならず芸術や社会的態度にも及んでいる同書は、日本文化のさまざまな面に対する欧米人の理解を深めた。

■known as 〜として知られる　■simultaneously 同時に　■undergo 経験する
■abbot 僧院長　■be appointed to 〜に任じられる　■collaborator 協力者

66 Yosano Akiko
Innovative Modern Poet

When the poet Yosano Tekkan began his own poetry group, they published the innovative and influential literary journal *Myojo* (translated as *Bright Star*, *Morning Star*, or *Evening Star* in English). *Myojo* appeared in three series: 1900-1908, 1921-1927, and 1947-1949. It was a sophisticated journal stressing visual arts, *tanka*, and Western-style poetry, and the **brilliance** of the contributing poets was a major influence on modern Japanese poetry.

Among its first contributors was Akiko. The two married in 1901, the same year that she published "Tangled Hair" (*Midaregami*), the first of her collections of poems. The collection included some 400 *tanka* poems of feminist sensuality and passion and they **were** very **warmly received**.

In addition to more volumes of poetry, she also published **commentary** on social issues, commentaries dealing with both classic and modern literature, and a translation of the *Tale of Genji* into modern Japanese. She also supported new poets and writers as they started out in the literary world. Together with nine other leading poets, she **compiled** the *Shin Man'yoshu* (*New Man'yoshu*) which contains 26,783 poems by 6,675 contributors between 1937 and 1939.

She died during World War II, and during the postwar years her works were basically ignored by the literary world and the general public. But her new poetry movement was important in the history of Japanese poetry. The energy and novel expression that she **infused into** classic poetry gradually became rediscovered and she is well regarded today. (240)

与謝野晶子

革新的な近代短歌の旗手

[1878-1942]

　歌人で詩人の与謝野鉄幹が立ち上げた詩歌結社（東京新詩社）は、革新的で影響力の大きい機関誌『明星』を発行する。『明星』は視覚芸術と短歌、西洋の訳詩に重点を置いた洗練された文芸誌で、1900〜1908年、1921〜1927年、1947〜1949年の第3次まで発行され、寄稿した歌人たちの優れた才能は近代日本の詩歌に大きな影響を与えた。

　最初の寄稿者の一人が与謝野晶子だ。晶子と鉄幹は1901年に結婚。同年、晶子は最初の歌集『みだれ髪』を出版した。この歌集には、フェミニズム的な思想を根底とする官能的で情熱的な短歌約400首が収録されており、大いに好評を博した。

　晶子は歌集以外にも、社会問題の評論や古典・現代文学の解説、『源氏物語』の現代語訳版などを次々に発表。さらに新進気鋭の歌人や作家を支援した。1937年から1939年にかけて刊行した『新万葉集』では、9人のそうそうたる歌人とともに選歌にあたり、6,675人による2万6,783首を収録した。

　晶子は第2次世界大戦中に亡くなり、戦後、その作品は文壇や大衆からほとんど顧みられることはなかったが、晶子による新しい詩歌運動は日本の詩の歴史において重要な意味を持った。晶子が古典的な短歌に吹き込んだエネルギーと斬新な表現は時を経て再発見されるようになり、晶子は今なお高い評価を受けている。

■ brilliance　才能　　■ be warmly received　温かく受け入れられる
■ commentary 評論　■ compile 編集する　■ infuse into 〜に吹き込む

67 Natsume Soseki

Deep in the Human Heart

Natsume Kinnosuke's early studies were in classical Chinese, but by the time he entered the University of Tokyo, he planned to become a scholar of English literature. At the university, he also began composing haiku **under the influence of** Masaoka Shiki, a life-long friend.

Sent to London as a **government-supported** student in 1900, he suffered from depression, stimulated by his **isolation** and economic situation. But he **devoted himself to** literary theory and literary criticism, and when he returned to Japan in 1903, he began teaching at the University of Tokyo.

Adopting the pen name Soseki, he wrote *I Am a Cat* (*Wagahai wa neko de aru*), *Botchan*, and *Grass for a Pillow* (*Kusamakura*). After **negotiating a contract** to publish novels **in installments** in the *Asahi* newspaper in 1907, he quit teaching and began writing full-time. He gained a broad audience with *Sore kara* (*And Then*), *Kokoro*, *Michikusa* (*Grass by the Wayside*), and his **incomplete masterpiece** *Meian* (*Light and Darkness*).

His works, especially *Kokoro*, portray the loneliness of modern man. *Kokoro* is set in 1912, when Japan was trying to deal with the contradictions between traditional society and **egotism** in human relationships in modern "civilized" society. The main figure feels displaced and finds only loneliness and solitude. It is a dark, lonely picture. This novel, his greatest literary achievement, presents a modern **everyman** we can recognize today.

While working on his last novel, he composed poems in classical Chinese every day. One of them expressed the idea of *sokuten kyoshi*, "to forsake the self and follow Heaven." One might say this expresses the true peace he longed for throughout his life. (269)

夏目漱石

現代人の孤独を深く描写
［1867-1916］

　夏目金之助は最初は漢詩文を学んでいたが、帝国大学（現・東京大学）に入学する頃には英文学者を目指すようになっていた。大学では、生涯の友となる正岡子規の影響で俳句を詠むようになる。

　1900年には官費でロンドン留学するが、孤立した生活と経済状況が引き金となってうつ状態に陥った。一方で文学論や文芸評論に力を入れ、1903年に帰国すると、東京帝国大学の講師となった。

　夏目漱石という筆名で『吾輩は猫である』『坊っちゃん』『草枕』を発表。1907年に朝日新聞で小説を連載する専属契約を結び、教師を辞めて本格的な執筆活動を始めた。『それから』『こころ』『道草』、そして未完の傑作『明暗』などで幅広い読者を獲得した。

　なかでも『こころ』は現代人の孤独を描いている。『こころ』の舞台は1912年。日本が、伝統的な社会と近代の「文明」社会の人間関係における自我との矛盾に葛藤していた時代であった。その主人公はどこにも居場所がない気持ちで孤独感を抱え、暗く、寂しい境遇にいる。漱石にとって最大の文学的功績となった同作は、どこにでもいるような現代人を表現しており、今日の私たちも自分を重ね合わせることができる。

　漱石は、自身にとって最後となる小説に取り組みながら、日々、漢詩を詠んだ。その中の一つに「己を捨てて天地自然に従う」境地を意味する「則天去私」がある。この言葉は、漱石が生涯求めてやまなかった真の平穏さを表しているといえるかもしれない。

■under the influence of 〜の影響を受けて　■government-supported 政府支援の　■isolation 孤立感　■devote oneself to 〜に専心する　■negotiate a contract 契約を結ぶ　■in installments 数回に分けて　■incomplete masterpiece 未完の傑作　■egotism 利己主義　■everyman ごく普通の人

68 Minakata Kumagusu
Folklorist and Biologist

This **polymath qualifies as** a biologist, an ethnologist, a naturalist, and a folklorist. In 1883 Minakata left Wakayama Prefecture for Tokyo, where he entered the preparatory school for the University of Tokyo. But he was less interested in studying in the classroom than in visiting zoos and botanical gardens, collecting animals and plants, and **transcribing** books in the library. He would maintain these habits the rest of his life.

Travelling by ship to California in 1886, he spent six months in San Francisco, before heading to Michigan. Learning that there were many undiscovered plants in Florida, in 1891, he headed there with microscopes, insect catchers, and a **plant press**, and began collecting specimens. From there he travelled to Cuba, Venezuela, and Jamaica, before heading to England. Spending time in the British Museum, other museums, and galleries, he developed friendships with people in different fields including anthropology, **archaeology**, and folklore.

Returning to Japan in 1900, he became involved in assisting Frederick Victor Dickens in translating the essay collection *Hojoki* into English. He continued his scientific research on **fungus** and **lichens** and discovered several varieties of **slime molds** (mycetozoa). He published **monographs** on natural history for the British journal *Nature* and on Japanese culture for the British folklore magazine *Notes and Queries*.

With the rise of Japanese folklore studies under Yanagita Kunio, Minakata also contributed articles in journals in support of protecting Japanese traditions. He also worked actively against the government's plans to **consolidate** local shrines into one single regional shrine, which he saw as a complete lack of respect for local customs. (261)

南方熊楠

民俗学と生物学の巨人

［1867-1941］

　博識家の南方熊楠は、生物学者、民族学者、博物学者、民俗学者と見なされている。南方は1883年に和歌山から上京し、東京大学予備門に入学した。しかし南方は、教室での勉強よりも、動物園や植物園を訪ねたり動物や植物を集めたりすることや、図書館で本を書き写したりすることへの関心が強かった。南方のこの習慣は生涯にわたって続いていく。

　1886年に船でカリフォルニア州に渡り、半年間サンフランシスコで過ごした後、ミシガン州に向かう。フロリダ州には多くの未発見の植物があることを知ると、1891年、顕微鏡、捕虫器、採集した植物を押し葉標本にする野冊を手に、同州で標本の採集を開始した。そこからキューバ、ベネズエラ、ジャマイカを経て渡英した南方は、大英博物館をはじめ、さまざまな博物館やギャラリーを訪ね、人類学や考古学、民俗学など多様な分野の人々と親交を深めた。

　1900年に帰国後、フレデリック・ヴィクター・ディキンズ（日本研究者）と『方丈記』の英訳（共訳）を進めるようになった。菌類や地衣類の科学的研究をも続け、数種類の粘菌類を発見。イギリスの科学学術誌『ネイチャー』では自然史の論文を、イギリスの民俗学誌『ノーツ・アンド・クエリーズ』では日本文化に関する論文を発表した。

　柳田国男によって日本の民俗学研究が盛んになると、南方も、日本の伝統を守る考えを支持して雑誌に寄稿。また、明治政府が発表した地方の神社を統合する政策は地方の風習への配慮が一切ないとして、激しい神社合祀反対運動を行った。

■polymath 博識家　　■qualify as 〜の基準を満たす　　■transcribe 書き写す
■plant press 野冊　　■archaeology 考古学　　■fungus 菌類　　■lichen 地衣類
■slime mold 粘菌類　　■monograph 研究論文　　■consolidate 合併する

69 Nishida Kitaro
Original Philosophy

Nishida Kitaro is arguably modern Japan's most important philosopher. He attempted to **assimilate** the philosophy and methodology of the West and used eastern religious tradition, especially Buddhism, as a base for his own thinking. Among his close friends was D. T. Suzuki, a prominent philosopher and promoter of Zen Buddhism.

After a period of studying on his own, he entered University of Tokyo as a special student and graduated in 1894. Facing financial **hardship** and family responsibilities, he began Zen meditation when he returned to teach at his **alma mater** in Kanazawa in 1896. During his ten years there, he developed material in psychology, logic, and ethics that went into his first major work, "An **Inquiry** into the Good" (*Zen no kenkyu*). This was his first **formulation** of "pure experience," which he **contended** was prior to all conceptions of subject and object, body and mind, spirit and matter.

While teaching at Kyoto University between 1910 and 1928, he extensively researched Western philosophy and Zen Buddhism. His work was the foundation of the Kyoto School of Philosophy. He began to view reality from a position close to **mysticism**, which he referred to as "absolute free will."

Nishida's work is recognized as the first **genuinely** original Japanese philosophy of the modern era and a stimulation to the original thinking of his **disciples**, many of whom became leading philosophers. Since translations of his works have been made in Western languages beginning in the 1950s, they have encouraged those who are looking for a more universal approach to philosophy that goes beyond conventional Western and Eastern ways of thinking. (264)

西田幾多郎

日本オリジナルの哲学を構築

［1870-1945］

　西田幾多郎は、近代日本哲学の第一人者といえる存在だ。西洋の哲学と
方法論を**取り込み**ながら、東洋の宗教的伝統、特に仏教を自身の思考の基
盤とした。親しい友人には、著名な哲学者で禅を広めた鈴木大拙（p.142）
がいた。

　独学の時期を経て、東京帝国大学（現・東京大学）に選科生として入学
し、1894年に卒業。経済的な**苦境**と家族を養う必要に迫られ、1896年に金
沢に戻り、**母校**の講師となり、この頃から座禅を始める。金沢での10年間
で心理学、論理学、倫理学に関する思索を深め、それは初の代表作『善の
研究』として結実する。これは「純粋経験」を初めて**体系化**したもので、
西田は、純粋経験は「主体と客体」、「心身」、「精神と物質」のすべての概
念より重要であると**主張**した。

　1910年から1928年まで京都帝国大学で教える間に西洋哲学と禅を徹底的
に研究。西田の著作は京都学派の哲学の基礎となった。西田は「絶対自由
の意志」とする**神秘主義**に近い立場から実在を捉えようとするようになっ
た。

　西田の著作は、近代日本において初となる**極めて**独創的な哲学として評
価され、**門弟**らも刺激を受けて独自の考えを生み、その多くが一流の哲学
者となった。1950年代以降、西田の著作がヨーロッパの言語に翻訳される
ようになってからは、従来の西洋・東洋の思考の枠組みを超え、哲学によ
り普遍的なアプローチを求める人々の支えとなってきた。

■assimilate 吸収する　■hardship 苦難　■alma mater 母校　■inquiry 探求
■formulation 公式化　■contend 強く主張する　■mysticism 神秘主義
■genuinely 純粋に　■disciple 弟子

70 Higuchi Ichiyo
Writing to Survive

Despite her **limited formal education** and family poverty, Higuchi Ichiyo became the most prominent woman writer of the Meiji period. Hiding her activity from her **disapproving** mother, she **immersed herself in** reading and in composing tanka, 31-syllable poems in classical style, and in 1886 she entered a poetry academy directed by the poet Nakajima Utako.

She began writing fiction and her first story dealt with the unhappy love of a boy and girl, a topic she often returned to in later works. It was published as "Yamizakura" (*Cherry Blossoms in the Dark*) in 1892. She continued to write stories but her publications brought little income.

She decided to give up writing, but after the family moved to a less expensive area near the Yoshiwara prostitution quarter, she gathered material for her best-received story, which was serialized as *Takekurabe*, "Comparing Heights". The story focused on the fate of a young woman **destined to** follow her older sister into the world of prostitution.

Moving to the Hongo district of Tokyo in 1894, she began teaching tanka and producing her best stories, inevitably dealing with the unhappy and limited lives of young women of her day. Overwork and economic struggles contributed to her early death from **tuberculosis**, at the age of 24.

One of the first female writers to **overcome** the **restrictions** of her age, her psychological treatment of characters, especially those on the verge of adolescence, is superb. *Tatekurabe* draws on an incident from *Ise monogatari* and Zeami's noh play *Izutsu* (The Well Curb). (252)

樋口一葉

生きるために小説家を志した女性作家

[1872-1896]

樋口一葉は正規の学校教育を途中までしか受けておらず、家も貧しかったにもかかわらず、明治を代表する女性作家となった。反対する母親に隠れて、読書や短歌に熱中して1886年には歌人の中島歌子が主宰する歌塾に入門した。

最初に書いた小説は少年少女の実らぬ恋をテーマにしたもので、一葉はその後の作品でも何度もこのテーマを取り上げている。この作品は1892年に『闇桜』として出版された。一葉は小説を書き続けたが、ほとんど収入にはならなかった。

小説を書くのを諦めようとしていたが、一家で吉原遊廓近くの物価の安い地域に引っ越し、一葉はここで小説の題材を集めた。そうして生まれた、一葉の作品として最も人気が高い作品が、連載小説の『たけくらべ』である。姉に続いて遊女になる定めにある若い女性の運命を描いている。

一葉は1894年に東京の本郷に移り住んで短歌を教えるようになり、代表作を次々に発表するようになる。作品のテーマは必ずと言っていいほど、当時の若い女性の不幸で制約の多い人生だった。一葉は長年の過労と経済的な苦労から結核を患い、24歳の若さで亡くなった。

女性作家の先駆けで、年齢の制約をはねのけた一葉が描いた中でも、特に思春期に差し掛かろうとしている登場人物の心理描写は秀逸である。『たけくらべ』は、『伊勢物語』や世阿弥（p.52）の能『井筒』から題材が取り入れられている。

■ limited 制限された　■ formal education 正規教育　■ disapproving 反対の
■ immerse oneself in 活動などに浸る　■ destined to ～する運命にある
■ tuberculosis 結核　■ overcome 克服する　■ restriction 制約

71 Uemura Shoen
Traditional Feminine Beauty

Daughter of a Kyoto tea merchant, Uemura Tsune was impressed by the woodblock prints of artists like Hokusai and was supported by her mother when she decided to pursue an artistic career. While upper-class women often **pursued** painting as a hobby after they married, however talented they might be, few made a career of painting. Those who did make it a career tended to live in Tokyo, rather in more conservative Kyoto, but with the support of her family, she studied with Suzuki Shonen, a landscape painter of the Chinese style, from whom the name Shoen was derived.

She later studied with a Takeuchi Seiho, a pioneer of modern *Nihonga*, Japanese-style painting, who was known for a refined style of **meticulous realism**. On a tour of Europe, he absorbed the influence of Turner and Corot, adding Western influences to his **repertoire**. This Western influence was passed on to Shoen.

Employing the resources and guidance available, Shoen's paintings of beautiful women began winning prizes in 1900, and she continued to focus on them as subjects. Traditional subjects make up a large portion of her work, but she is considered a major innovator in the *bijin-ga* genre, although she used it to **depict** the traditional beauty standards of women in a time when the status of women was slowly changing.

In 1941 she became a member of the Imperial Art Academy and three years later she became a court artist, *teishitsu gigeiin*. In 1948 she became the first woman to receive the **Order of Culture**. (253)

上村松園

伝統的な女性美を日本画で描写

[1875-1949]

　京都の葉茶屋の娘として生まれた上村津禰、のちの松園は、北斎（p.98）をはじめとする浮世絵師の版画に感銘を受け、母の後押しを受けて絵の道に進んだ。当時、上流階級の女性が結婚して趣味で絵を描くことは多かったが、どれほど才能があっても絵を描くことを職業にした女性はほとんどいなかった。保守的な京都より東京に住む画家が多かったが、松園は家族の協力を得て、山水画を得意とした鈴木松年に師事。松園の名前は松年に由来している。

　その後、近代日本画の先駆者で、洗練された**写実画法**で知られた竹内栖鳳に師事。栖鳳は欧州を訪れた際にターナーやコローの作風に感化され、西洋画の影響を加えた**作品**を制作する。この西洋画の影響は松園にも受け継がれた。

　松園は自身の能力と教わったことを生かし、1900年頃には美人画が（美術展で）入賞するようになり、その後も女性を題材にした作品を描き続けた。松園の題材の大半が伝統的なもので、女性の地位が徐々に変わりつつあった時代に女性の昔ながらの美の基準を**表現**していたが、松園は美人画のジャンルで主要な革新者と見なされた。

　1941年には帝国芸術院会員、3年後には皇室の美術・工芸品を制作する美術家、帝室技芸員となる。1948年には女性として初めて**文化勲章**を受章した。

■pursue 追い求める　■meticulous 細部まで精確な　■realism 写実主義
■repertoire レパートリー　■depict 描写する　■Order of Culture 文化勲章

72 Noguchi Hideyo
Sacrifices for Medicine

Born into a poor farm family in northern Japan, despite being **unable to afford** new textbooks, Noguchi Hideyo excelled at school. With support from a **mentor**, he continued his education in better schools. Having suffered a bad burn on his left hand as a child, he underwent an operation and was so impressed with medical science that he chose medicine as a career.

He became a **live-in** medical student at a regional hospital where he had been operated on, and then moved to Tokyo, where he passed the first half of the **medical practitioner**'s exam within the first year. He passed the second half within the next year, and received his **medical license** at the age of twenty.

He decided to devote himself to **bacteriology** and to using what he learned for the public good. In 1900 he went to America and worked as a research assistant at various institutions before receiving an appointment at the Rockefeller Institute for Medical Research, where he succeeded in cultivating the bacteria that causes **syphilis**.

In 1918 he went to Central and South America to study a **pandemic outbreak** of yellow fever in hopes of developing a vaccine. When a research colleague died of yellow fever in Africa, he went there for research in 1927 intending to stay only a short time. However he extended his stay into 1928, believing that he was close to discovering methods for treating the disease. As he was preparing to return to the United States, he himself contracted yellow fever and died at the age of fifty one. (254)

野口英世

細菌研究に身を捧げた医師

[1876-1928]

　北日本（東北・福島）の貧しい農家に生まれた野口英世(のぐちひでよ)は、新しい教科書を買う余裕もなかったが、学校（尋常小学校）では優秀な成績を収めた。恩師の援助を受け、より良い学校（高等小学校）で教育を受ける。子どもの頃に左手に大やけどを負って手術を受けた野口は、医学の力に感銘を受け、その道に進むことを選ぶ。

　手術をしてもらった医院に書生として住み込み、上京して1年で医術開業試験の前期試験に合格。翌年には後期試験に合格し、20歳で医師免許を取得した。

　細菌学の研究に専念し、学んだことを公益のために役立てようと決意。1900年に渡米し、いくつかの機関で研究助手を務めた後、ロックフェラー医学研究所に勤め、梅毒(ばいどく)の病原体である梅毒スピロヘータ菌の培養に成功した。

　1918年には、黄熱病のワクチン開発を目指し、その研究のため、黄熱病が大流行していた中南米（エクアドル）に渡った。1927年、研究を行うために短期滞在するつもりでアフリカを訪れていた際に研究仲間が現地で黄熱病で亡くなったが、野口は、間もなく治療法を発見できると信じ、1928年まで滞在期間を延長。アメリカに戻る準備をしていたときに、自身も黄熱病に感染し、51歳で亡くなった。

■be unable to afford 買う余裕がない　■mentor 指導者　■live-in 住み込みの
■medical practitioner 医師　■medical license 医師免許　■bacteriology 細菌学　■syphilis 梅毒　■pandemic outbreak 病気などの世界的流行

73 Yoshino Sakuzo

Defining Sovereignty

While studying at the prestigious Second Higher School in Sendai, Yoshino converted to Christianity, before going on to the University of Tokyo. After two years of graduate study, he became the tutor of the eldest son of Yuan Shikai (En Seigai), an official of the Qing dynasty who later became president of the new Republic of China.

After returning to Japan, Yoshino became a professor of law at the University of Tokyo. He became renowned for his 1916 article "On the Meaning of Constitutional Government and the Methods to Perfect It" (*Kensei no hongi o toite sono yushu no bi o nasu no michi o ronzu*). In this work he held that even if **sovereignty** lay in the imperial institution, under the Meiji Constitution, it was still possible to have a responsible representative government elected by the people.

His interpretation was that constitutional government was based upon *minpon shugi*, literally "people as the base." He **differentiated** this from *minshu shugi*, which is the usual translation of "democracy," meaning "popular sovereignty." He believed that the government should act on behalf of the popular welfare and that the people should be the ultimate judge, by voting in elections and through responsible cabinets. His commitment to people as the base of constitutional government made him the leading spokesman for liberal Taisho democracy.

In addition to advocating political reform, self-rule for Japan's colonies, and social welfare policies, he supported legal recognition for labor unions and legislation to regulate labor-employee relations. Significantly, he opposed **interference** in politics by non-parliamentary powers including the House of Peers, the Genro (elder statesmen), and the **military high command**. (269)

吉野作造

民本主義を唱えた論客

[1878-1933]

　吉野作造は仙台の名門校、第二高等学校在学中にキリスト教に入信し、東京帝国大学に進学。同大学（院）で2年間学び、（中国に渡り）のちに中華民国初代大総統となる清の官僚、袁世凱に中国に招かれ長男の家庭教師を務めた。

　（ヨーロッパ留学を経て）帰国後、東京帝国大学法科大学教授に就任。

　1916年に発表した評論「憲政の本義を説いて其有終の美を済すの途を論ず」で名を成した。同評論で吉野は、たとえ主権が天皇にあるとしても、明治憲法の下では、国民によって選ばれた責任ある代議制の責任政府を持つことは可能であると主張した。

　吉野は、立憲政治は「民本主義」に基づくものであると考え、国民主権を意味する民主主義とは区別していた。政府は国民の利福のために行動すべきであり、選挙での投票や責任ある内閣を通じて最終的な判断は国民に委ねられるべきだと考え、立憲政治の基本は国民にあるとし、自由主義的な大正デモクラシーの代表的な論客となった。

　吉野は政治改革や植民地の自治、社会福祉政策を提唱し、労働組合の合法化や労使関係を規定する法の制定を支持した。重要なのは、貴族院や元老院、軍の首脳部など、（公選の）議会外の権力者が政治に干渉するのに異議を唱えたことである。

■sovereignty 主権　■differentiate 区別する　■interference 干渉　■military high command 軍の首脳部

74 Yoshida Shigeru
Prime Minister Who Constructed Postwar Japan

Having served as a prewar diplomat in China, Italy, and Great Britain, beginning in 1939 Yoshida Shigeru **sat out** the war years as an ordinary citizen. After World War II, his record as an "internationalist" helped him to **win acceptance** with the Allied Occupation. He served as foreign minister briefly before taking on the duties of prime minister from 1946 to 1954. He would become the most famous politician of postwar Japan, leading the country to **restored sovereignty** in 1952.

Yoshida believed that the militarists had interrupted an earlier movement toward democracy. He contended that the Occupation simply needed to expel the militarists, stimulate the economy, and help reestablish Japan as a participating member of the international community.

Tough with leftists and the trade unions, he **was** also **stubborn with** the Americans. He **rankled** Occupation authorities with his view that the key to making Japan independent, economically stable, and politically centralized was to leave the process to Japanese big business, **bureaucrats**, and conservative politicians.

Through the "Yoshida era" he **oversaw** the strengthening of the economic, military, and technological relationship between Japan and the United States. At the same time, one of his primary objectives was to sign a peace treaty and end the Occupation. Although he fell from power with the return of purged politicians, his influence continued. The politicians of the so-called "Yoshida school" (*Yoshida gakko*) who led Japan into the 1980s included Ikeda Hayato and Sato Eisaku. (244)

吉田茂

戦後日本を築いた首相
［1878-1967］

　戦前、中国、イタリア、イギリスで領事・大使を務めた吉田茂（よしだしげる）は、1939年からは在野の人として戦時中を過ごした。第2次世界大戦後は「国際主義者」としてのキャリアを生かし、占領軍に受け入れられた。短期間、外相に就任した後、1946年から1954年まで首相を務めた。1952年には日本の主権回復を導き、戦後の日本で最も有名な政治家となった。

　吉田は、戦前の民主主義運動をつぶしたのは軍国主義者だと考えており、占領軍司令部は軍国主義者を一掃して経済を活性化させ、日本を再建させて国際社会に仲間入りさせることを必要としていると主張した。

　吉田は左翼や労働組合には断固たる態度で臨み、アメリカにも同じく譲らなかった。日本を独立させ、経済的な安定をもたらし、政治の中央集権化を果たす鍵（かぎ）は、そのプロセスを日本の大企業や官僚、保守派の政治家に任せることだと唱え、占領軍司令部をいら立たせた。

　「吉田時代（首相時代）」には、日米間の経済・軍事・技術面での関係強化を統括した。それとともに吉田が目指したことは、講和条約の締結と占領終結だった。追放された議員らが返り咲いたことなどもあり権力の座からは降りたが、吉田は影響力を振るい続けた。「吉田学校」出身で1980年代に至るまで日本を牽引した政治家には池田勇人（いけだはやと）、佐藤栄作（さとうえいさく）らがいる。

■sat out 〜が過ぎ去るのを待つ　■win acceptance 受け入れられる　■restore 回復する　■sovereignty 主権　■tough with 〜に厳しい　■be stubborn with 〜に断固とした態度を取る　■rankle 苦しめる　■bureaucrat 官僚　■oversee 管理する

75 Kitaoji Rosanjin
Aesthetically Presented Cuisine

This legendary **Renaissance man** once declared, "If clothes make the person, dishes make the food." He meant that if the **container** does not have the appropriate size, depth, color, and design to harmonize with food, it **detracts from** the total appeal of the meal. The visual appeal of the vessels must contribute to the taste.

Rosanjin began as a calligrapher before studying Kutani **porcelain** production in Kanazawa. He moved to Kita-Kamakura, built his own kiln, and began to create pottery. Convinced that the ceramics that were available in his day were inadequate, he wanted to change that. To do this, he recruited potters **versed in** different styles and ordered clay from around Japan to produce vessels in his studio that matched cuisine. He did so by imitating a broad assortment of earlier Japanese **earthenwares**, until he was able to develop his own individual, contemporary style.

Before World War II, most of his production was inspired by blue-and-white Imari ware and overglaze enamel Kutani ware. Following the war, however, he shifted to several older stoneware such as Bizen and Mino wares. He became especially attached to Oribe, from Gifu Prefecture, which is the style that **prompted** the national government to **designate** him as a **Living National Treasure**, an honor he declined to accept.

It would be wrong to classify him among the current-day "celebrity chefs," because he was **multi-faceted**. He possessed skills as a calligrapher, a potter, a lacquerware craftsman, and a chef, **excelling at** each and combining them in just the right way. (253)

北大路魯山人

食を極めた多才な教養人

[1883-1959]

　ルネサンス的（多才な）教養人として知られた北大路魯山人は、かつて「食器は料理の着物である」と明言している。器の大きさ、深さ、色、デザインが料理と調和していなければ、その料理全体のおいしさが損なわれるとして、器の視覚的な魅力も料理の味を支えなければならないと説いた。

　元は書家だった魯山人は、金沢で九谷焼きを学び、その後、北鎌倉に移り住み、自分の窯を設け、作陶を始めた。当時の焼き物に物足りなさを感じ、現状を変えたいと考えた魯山人は、さまざまな技法に精通した陶芸家を招き、全国から土を取り寄せ、料理に合わせた器を工房で制作。多種多様な日本の古陶器を模倣しながら、独自の現代的なスタイルを確立していった。

　第2次世界大戦前の魯山人は、白磁に青で染付した伊万里焼や上絵付けが特徴の九谷焼から作品の着想を得ていたが、戦後は備前焼や美濃焼などの古磁器に関心を移していった。特に愛着を持ったのが岐阜県の織部焼だ。魯山人はそれにより、織部焼の重要無形文化財保持者（人間国宝）にも推挙されたが、辞退した。

　マルチな才能を持っていたからといって、魯山人を現在の有名シェフと同等に捉えるのは間違った見方かもしれない。魯山人は書家、陶芸家、漆芸家、そして料理人としても秀で、それぞれの領域を絶妙に組み合わせた。

■Renaissance man ルネサンス的教養人　■container 器　■detract from 〜を損なう　■porcelain 磁器　■versed in 〜を熟知している　■earthenware 陶器　■prompt 促す　■designate 指名する　■Living National Treasure 人間国宝　■multi-faceted マルチな　■excel at 〜に秀でる

76 Tanizaki Junichiro
Contemporary Versions of Tradition

Tanizaki's **sensual** approach to life touched on masochism, lesbianism, **lust, fetishes**, and triangular relationships. He wrote stories about men who find their ultimate happiness in total devotion to women who are either **unapproachably** pure or extremely proud and cruel. These men experience humiliation and allow themselves to be **subjugated**, yet this **elevates** them **to** an almost religious undefiled state.

Moving from Tokyo to the more traditional Kansai area at the time of the Great Tokyo Earthquake of 1923, Tanizaki was inspired by pure forms of Japanese culture there. During World War II, he avoided current events and **leaned toward** his own imagination, especially inspired by traditions from the Heian period.

In 1939 he began a contemporary Japanese **rendering** of *Genji Monogatari*. This long-term project probably prompted him to start writing *The Makioka Sisters* (*Sasameyuki*) in 1942. This novel is an elegy to a beautiful era that has already passed. The novel began serialization in 1943, was halted during the last years of the war, and was not completed until 1948.

Tanizaki's short stories *The Mother of Captain Shigemoto* (*Shosho Shigemoto no Haha*, 1950) and *The Key* (*Kagi*, 1956) take up, respectively, the theme of love between mother and son and the theme of sexual struggle leading to **dominance**. In one of his last novels, *Diary of a Mad Old Man* (*Futen rojin nikki,* 1962), he combined the themes of the femme fatale and the mother figure to bring the main character of the story to a final, if troubled, kind of **salvation**. (251)

谷崎潤一郎

伝統を現代的に解釈

［1886-1965］

　谷崎 潤一郎の作品では、マゾヒズム、女性間の同性愛、情欲、フェティ
シズム、三角関係をテーマに、人生に対する**官能的な**アプローチで、**近寄
りがたい**ほど純粋か、極めて高慢で冷酷な女性に徹底的に尽くすことを至
福と考える男性たちが描かれている。谷崎が描くこうした男性たちは屈辱
を味わい、**服従を受け入れる**が、それによって宗教的と言ってよいほどの
汚れのない**高みに上り詰める**。

　1923年の関東大震災を機に東京から関西に移り住んだ谷崎は、その地に
純粋な形で残っている日本文化に刺激を受けた。第2次世界大戦中は、目
の前で起こっている出来事ではなく、特に平安時代の伝統に着想を得て想
像の世界に**傾倒**していった。

　1939年、谷崎は『源氏物語』の**現代語訳**に取り掛かる。おそらくこの長
期的なプロジェクトをきっかけに、1942年には、過ぎ去った美しい時代へ
のエレジー、『細雪』の執筆を開始する。同作品は1943年に連載が始まり、
終戦前に中断し、1948年に完成した。

　谷崎の短編小説『少 将 滋幹の母』（1950年）では母と息子の愛、『鍵』
（1956年）では性的な**優位性**をめぐる闘いをテーマにしている。晩年の小
説の一つ、『瘋癲老人日記』（1962年）では、魔性の女と理想の母親像とい
うテーマを組み合わせ、主人公が苦しみながらも最終的に一種の救いを得
る様を描いている。

■sensual 官能的な　■lust 肉欲　■fetish フェティッシュ　■unapproachably
近寄りがたい　■subjugate 服従させる　■elevate … to …を～に高める　■lean
toward ～に傾く　■render 訳す　■dominance 支配　■salvation 救済

77 Hiratsuka Raicho
Advocate for Women

A graduate of Japan Women's University, Hiratsuka Haru **aroused public censure** when she planned to **commit double suicide** with her married teacher Morita Sohei. The pair were found alive in the mountains of Nasu Shiobara.

In the 1910s and 1920s she challenged **male-defined social norms**, taking a radical feminist position. Adopting the pen name Raicho, "Thunderbird," she became a founding member of the *Seitosha*, the Blue Stocking Society, which aimed at the development of women's talents.

In the literary magazine they published, called *Seito* (Blue Stocking), she introduced a manifesto entitled "In the Beginning Woman Was the Sun" (*Genshi josei wa taiyo de atta*), a reference to Amaterasu, the Sun Goddess, and the spiritual independence that women had lost. The magazine published works by feminist Yosano Akiko and Raicho's critique of "good wife, wise mother" (*ryosai kenbo*), the **conventional view** of the proper role for women in male-dominated society.

Leaving home in 1914 to live with the painter Okumura Hiroshi, she gave birth to a daughter and a son. In 1920 she joined Ichikawa Fusae and others in forming the *Shin Fujin Kyokai*, New Woman's Association, a movement to raise the social and legal position of women.

During World War II, she refused to support the **militarist** state and following the war, she resumed campaigning for women's rights and for peace. She became the first president of the Federation of Japanese Women's Societies, *Nihon Fujin Dantai Rengokai*, and continued to write, lecture, and **advocate for** peace and women's rights until her death. (252)

平塚らいてう

女性解放運動家

[1886-1971]

　平塚明は、日本女子大学校（現・日本女子大学）を卒業し、結婚していた教師の森田草平と**心中**未遂を起こして那須塩原の山中で救助され、**世間から非難を浴びた。**

　1910年代から1920年代にかけて、**男性によって決められる社会規範**に異議を唱え、急進的なフェミニストとしての立場を取った。「雷鳥」を意味する筆名らいてうを名乗り、女性の人材育成を目指す団体、青鞜社の立ち上げメンバーとなった。

　文芸誌『青鞜』の発刊の辞として、太陽の女神である天照大神と女性が失った精神的自立に言及し、「元始、女性は実に太陽であった」という文章を寄せた。同誌には、女性解放論者の与謝野晶子（p.144）の作品や、男性優位社会における**伝統的な女性観**である「良妻賢母」を批判したらいてうの作品も掲載された。

　1914年に家を出て画家の奥村博史と同棲し、娘1人と息子1人を出産。1920年、市川房江（p.174）らと女性の社会的・法的権利獲得を目指す団体「新婦人協会」を発足した。

　第2次世界大戦中は、**軍国主義**を支持することを拒否し、戦後は女性解放運動と反戦運動を再開。日本婦人団体連合会の初代会長に就任し、執筆や講演を続け、亡くなるまで反戦と女性の**権利獲得**を提唱した。

■arouse 喚起する　■public censure 世論の批判　■commit double suicide 心中する　■male-defined 男性が定義する　■social norms 社会規範　■conventional view 型にはまった見方　■militarist 軍国主義的な　■advocate for 〜を提唱する

78 Yamaoka Magokichi
Efficiency for Farmers

Leaving his isolated farming village in 1903, Yamaoka Magokichi found work in pipe installation at Osaka Gas company, where he **accumulated** experience at small factory work sites, learning the principles and construction of engines.

He **started up** his own gas pipe installation and equipment sales business. With a few employees, he purchased old gas engines, **renovated** them, and sold them at attractive prices. In 1912, he founded a repair shop, under the company name *Yamaoka Hatsudoki Kosakusho*, which is now Yanmar.

Yamaoka realized that urban areas could supply electric power but that farmers would still depend on gas engines. Discovering that small gas engines converted to oil engines were being used to power **rice hulling machines**, he began building engine prototypes for agricultural uses. After successfully manufacturing small oil-powered rice hulling machines, he developed a small engine to pump water from **irrigation canals**.

Attending a major trade show in Leipzig, Germany, he **headed straight for** the engine exhibit, which showed a film for a manufacturer named MAN (Maschinenfabrik Augsburg-Nurnberg AG) showing the world's first diesel engine. Realizing that diesel engines were durable, and fuel costs were only one-fourth that of oil engines, he immediately began designing small diesels to power farming machinery.

Japan already imported engines patented by Rudolf Diesel, but they were heavy 250 hp engines. Determining that a small 3-5 hp engine would **be sufficient for** farm work, his engineers set to work in building smaller ones. When they succeeded in 1933, the small inexpensive Yanmar engines became a means of significantly reducing the labor of farming, mountain, and fishing villages throughout the country. (266)

山岡孫吉

農家を助けるディーゼルエンジンを開発

［1888-1962］

　山岡孫吉は、1903年に辺ぴな農村を出て、大阪瓦斯で配管工事の仕事に就き、小さな工場の現場で経験を積みながらエンジンの原理や構造を学んだ。

　その後、ガス管工事とガス器具販売を始め、数人の従業員と古いガスエンジンを買い取って修理し、手頃な値段で販売。1912年、山岡発動機工作所（現・ヤンマーホールディングス）の名で修理工場を立ち上げた。

　山岡は、都市部では電力を供給できるが、農家が使用しているのはいまなおガスエンジンが主であることに着目する。小型のガスエンジンを石油エンジンに改造したものが籾すり機の動力源に使われていることを知り、農業用エンジンを試作。石油で動く小型の籾すり機の製造に成功すると、用水路の水を汲み上げる小型エンジンを開発した。

　その後ドイツのライプツィヒで大きな見本市に参加した山岡がまっすぐ向かった先は、エンジンの展示場だった。そこで、世界初のディーゼルエンジンを開発したマン社の映画を見て、ディーゼルエンジンは耐久性があり、燃費が石油エンジンの4分の1で済むことを知ると、山岡はただちに農機具用の小型ディーゼルエンジンの設計を始めた。

　日本にはすでに、技術者ルドルフ・ディーゼルの特許があるエンジンが輸入されていたが、250馬力もあり、重かった。農作業には3〜5馬力の小型エンジンで十分だと判断した山岡の技術者らは、より小型のエンジンの開発に取り掛かる。1933年についにディーゼルエンジンの小型化に成功。小型で安価なヤンマーのエンジンは、日本全国の農作業や山村、漁村の作業の労力を大幅に削減した。

■ accumulate 蓄積する　■ start up 開業する　■ renovate 修理する　■ rice hulling machine 籾すり機　■ irrigation canal 用水路　■ head straight for 〜へ直行する　■ be sufficient for 〜には十分である

79 Yanagi Muneyoshi
The Beauty of Handcrafts

Yanagi Muneyoshi, also known as Yanagi Soetsu, found beauty in **implements** used in daily life that had largely **been ignored by** other people. He developed a strong interest in the creative abilities of the common people, coining the word *mingei*, folk crafts, to describe beauty that was the product of **anonymous** craftmanship. Yanagi contended that *mingei* differed from *bijutsu*, fine art, which was created for aesthetic appreciation alone, not for practical use.

He preferred the term folk craft to folk art, because the former emphasized the **utilitarian** function. European art historians, he felt, emphasized only individual artists, while overlooking the **collective genius** of groups working together. Further, beauty was not always the result of any conscious intent. Often it was born of sheer chance and the **accumulated** skills of generations.

Yanagi's aesthetics attracted the British potter Bernard Leach and the Japanese potters Hamada Shoji and Kawai Kanjiro. They worked together to inspire a movement for the appreciation of the decorative arts including pottery and textiles. As leading spokesman for the Japanese folk-craft movement, Yanagi believed that handcrafted objects could possess **artistic merit** even if they were functional and were produced in quantity for daily use. He was attracted to the simple beauty of objects by craftspeople who saw their work not as a form of self-expression, but as a plain job.

A major contribution of Yanagi and his **cohorts** was the establishment of the Japan Folk-Craft Museum in Tokyo in 1936. Its displays include fabrics, ceramics, metalware, and furniture, which reflect regional and ethnic distinctions. (255)

柳宗悦

手仕事に美を見いだした民芸運動の父

［1889-1961］

　柳宗悦とも呼ばれた柳宗悦は、あまり**顧みられる**ことのなかった日常で使われる**道具**に美を見いだした。庶民の創造力に強い関心を抱き、**名もない**職人たちの技が生み出す美を表すために「民芸」という言葉を造語。民芸は、実用的な用途ではなく審美的な鑑賞のみを目的とした「美術」という言葉とは異なものと主張した。

　柳は、民芸を英語で表す際、フォーク・アート（folk art）ではなく、**実用的な機能**の意味合いが強いフォーク・クラフト（folk craft）という言葉を好んだ。柳から見れば、欧州の美術史家は、個人の芸術家のみを取り上げ、集団による「**集合天才**（多くの才能の集結）」をないがしろにしていた。さらに、美とは必ずしも意図して生まれるわけではなく、多くの場合は偶然の産物で、何世代にもわたって**蓄積された技**の賜物だというのが柳の考えだった。

　柳の美意識に引かれたイギリスの陶芸家、バーナード・リーチや日本の陶芸家、濱田庄司、河井寛次郎らはともに、陶芸や織物をはじめとする装飾芸術を鑑賞する動きを盛り立てていく。日本の民芸運動の中心人物となった柳は、手仕事で生まれた道具には、それが日用品として大量生産される機能的なものであっても**芸術的な価値**が宿り得ると考え、自分の作ったものを自己表現とは捉えず、単なる仕事と見なしていた職人たちの手による道具のシンプルな美しさに引かれた。

　柳とその**賛同者**らの大きな貢献は、1936年に東京に日本民芸館を設立したことである。同館では、地域性や民族性の違いが出ている織物、陶磁器、金属製品、家具などを展示している。

■ implement（複数形で）道具　　■ be ignored by ～に顧みられない
■ anonymous 名もない、ありふれた　■ utilitarian 実用的な　■ collective genius
集合天才　■ accumulated 積み重ねられた　■ artistic merit 芸術的価値
■ cohort 仲間

80 Akutagawa Ryunosuke
Psychological Insight

Akutagawa initiated his publishing career while **majoring in** English literature at the University of Tokyo. His first series of stories was based on the *Konjaku monogatari* collection, Japanese tales from the twelfth and thirteenth centuries, but they had a modern, **psychological insight**.

His short story "Hana" ("The Nose") describes a high-ranking Buddhist priest who is troubled by his huge nose, finds a way to reduce its size, **is derided for** doing this, and then returns the nose to its original size. Despite the simple theme, the insight into human nature attracted the attention of the great writer Natsume Soseki.

Akutagawa's most accomplished works include *Rashomon* ("Rashomon"), *Yabu no naka* ("In a Grove"), *Kumo no ito* ("The Spider's Thread") and *Jigokuhen* ("Hell Screen"). The first two of these became sources of the movie *Rashomon* by Kurosawa Akira. The last of the four **takes up** the question of what sacrifices an artist must make in order to create his art.

He continued to borrow material from old tales, recreating them in terms of contemporary psychology, and employing sophisticated literary devices, sometimes drawn from Western sources.

Toward the end of his life, he produced a tale about a creature from Japanese folklore titled *Kappa* ("Kappa"), which **satirizes** contemporary society in a way that we can grasp even today. His *Haguruma* ("Cogwheel") is a terrifying account of an exceptionally sensitive mind that is gradually breaking apart. Akutagawa himself was afraid that he had inherited his mother's mental disorder and he **committed suicide** at the age of 35 in 1927. (255)

芥川龍之介

心理描写に長けた小説家

［1892-1927］

芥川龍之介は東京帝国大学英文科在籍中に小説を書き始めた。初期の作品は、12～13世紀の日本の説話『今昔物語集』を下敷きに、現代的な心理的な洞察を加えた小説だ。

短編『鼻』は、長鼻に悩む高僧が鼻を小さくする方法を見つけるが、周囲に嘲笑されて鼻を元の大きさに戻す様子を描いた話で、シンプルでありながら、人間の本質に対する洞察力に満ちたテーマで、文豪・夏目漱石（p.146）に認められた。

代表作は『羅生門』『藪の中』『蜘蛛の糸』『地獄変』など。最初の2作品を下敷きに、黒澤明（p.194）は『羅生門』として映画化している。『地獄変』は、芸術家は作品を生み出すためにどこまで犠牲を払うべきなのかという問題に焦点を当てている。

芥川は、昔話の素材を借用し、時には西洋の文学も基にしながら、そうした物語を現代の心理学的な観点から再構成し、洗練された文学的な工夫を凝らしている。

晩年には、日本の民話に出てくる生き物を題名にした『河童』を発表し、今日の私たちにも通じる方法で現代社会を風刺した。『歯車』は、極めて繊細な人物が次第に壊れていく恐ろしい様を表現した話である。芥川は、精神を病んでいた母親の性質を自身が受け継いでいるのではないかと恐れ、1927年に35歳で自殺した。

■major in ～専攻する　■psychological insight 心理的洞察力　■be derided for ～でばかにされる　■take up ～に取り組む　■satirize 風刺する　■commit suicide 自殺する

81 Ichikawa Fusae
Equality for Women

Switching from teaching elementary school to becoming the first woman reporter for the newspaper *Nagoya Shimbun*, Ichikawa Fusae **became concerned with** both labor and feminist issues. Between 1919 and 1920 she worked with Hiratsuka Raicho and others in establishing the New Women's Association (*Shin Fujin Kyokai*) to raise the social and political position of women in Japan. Four years later, she helped found the Women's Suffrage League (*Fusen Kakutoku Domei*).

For the next 16 years, as the leading figure in the women's **suffrage** movement, she tried to persuade liberal politicians to support legislation that would **grant** political rights to women.

Following the end of the Second World War, in 1945, she organized and became president of the New Japan Women's League (Shin Nihon Fujin Domei), an organization that aimed at improving the **legal status** of women. **Ironically**, she **was banned from** public office because of associations with state-sponsored women's organizations during the war.

Following the end of the Occupation, she resigned from women's organizations in 1953, and on the basis of her constant campaigns for social equality and against political corruption, she was elected to the House of Councillors as an independent. **With the exception of** 1971-1974, she remained in the Diet until her death. (206)

市川房枝

女性の地位向上に尽力

［1893-1981］

　小学校教員から名古屋新聞（現・中日新聞）初の女性記者となった市川
房枝は、労働問題と婦人運動に**関心を持つ**ようになる。1919年から1920年
にかけて、平塚らいてう（p.166）らとともに新婦人協会を設立し、日本に
おける女性の社会的・政治的地位の向上に尽力。4年後には婦人参政権獲
得期成同盟会（婦選獲得同盟）の結成に協力する。

　以後16年間、女性**参政権**運動の第一人者として、女性に政治的権利を**与
える**法律を支持するようリベラルな政治家に働き掛けた。

　第2次世界大戦の終結後、1945年に女性の**法的地位**の向上を目指した新
日本婦人同盟を結成し、会長に就任した。**皮肉**にも市川は戦時中に国策に
協力した婦人団体との関係を問われ、一時、公職**追放**となる。

　占領が終了した1953年には女性団体を辞し、社会的平等と政治汚職に反
対する運動を続けていたことから参議院議員選挙に無所属で出馬し当選。
1971年から1974年（落選期間）を**除き**、亡くなるまで国会議員を務めた。

■ become concerned with 〜と関係する　■ suffrage 参政権　■ grant 与える
■ legal status 法的地位　■ ironically 皮肉にも　■ be banned from 〜を禁じら
れる　■ with the exception of 〜を例外として

82 Matsushita Konosuke
Contributing to Society

After opening a small electric **fixture** shop in Osaka in 1918, Matsushita Konosuke was quickly successful in producing small battery-powered bicycle lamps. From that small beginning, he expanded his business into a home appliance factory, which produced a wide variety of electric products to make daily life convenient and comfortable.

After reorganizing his business as Matsushita Electric Industrial Company, Ltd., he began to develop **tie-ups with** the European electric manufacturer Philips. Constantly seeking innovations and better products, he turned his company into the **front-running** Japanese manufacturer of home appliances. The company **instituted** mass-production methods at a highly **opportune** time. From the late 1950s into the next decade, there was a boom in Japanese society for home electronics.

Leading his company to impressive domestic growth by marketing washing machines, refrigerators, and televisions, he then turned to exports. Under the brand name "National," these products became internationally popular.

While Matsushita became a successful and wealthy man—having the highest personal income in Japan in 1952—he stuck with traditional Japanese management practices in the company. He **launched** the "Peace and Happiness through Prosperity" (PHP) movement right after World War II came to an end. Through this he **advocated** a positive philosophy of contributing to society and **well-being** through both cultural and business activities. His philosophy and management style remain popular topics in books targeted at businesspeople. (224)

松下幸之助

家電で日本社会に貢献

[1894-1989]

松下幸之助は、1918年に大阪で小さな電気器具製作所を開業し、小型自転車用電池ランプの製造にいち早く成功した。その小さな一歩から、すぐに事業を家電製造工場へと拡大し、日常生活を便利で快適にするさまざまな電気製品を生産した。

松下電器産業株式会社（現・パナソニックグループ）として事業を再編成してからは、欧州の電機メーカーであるフィリップスと**提携**。常に革新的でより良い製品を追い求め、自身の会社を、日本を**代表**する家電メーカーへと成長させた。これを**好機**に大量生産方式を**導入**。1950年代後半から1960年代にかけて、日本には家電ブームが到来した。

洗濯機、冷蔵庫、テレビなどを売り出し、国内で目覚ましい成長を遂げると、松下は輸出にも目を向け、「ナショナル」というブランド名で販売した製品は世界的に人気を博した。

松下は、1952年には長者番付で全国1位になるほどの富豪となって成功を収めるが、自社では日本の伝統的な経営手法を守り続けた。第2次世界大戦の終戦直後には、PHP（「事業活動の繁栄によって社会の平和と幸福を達成しよう」という意味）運動を**開始**し、文化活動と企業活動の両面から社会と人々の幸福に**貢献**するポジティブな理念を提唱した。ビジネスパーソンを対象とした書籍では、松下の哲学や経営スタイルは今なお人気を呼んでいる。

■ fixture 設備　■ tie-ups with 〜との提携　■ front-running 首位の　■ institute 始める　■ opportune 時宜を得た　■ launch 始める　■ advocate 提唱する　■ well-being 幸福

83 Miyazawa Kenji
Empathy and Nature

Miyazawa Kenji was born in a rural village in Iwate Prefecture, and grew up in a **prosperous, pious** Buddhist family of pawnbrokers. Unwilling to succeed to the business of earning money from poor farmers pawning their **meager** possessions and disagreeing with his father over religious beliefs, Miyazawa turned to teaching and then to writing.

He published his collection of children's stories titled "The Restaurant of Many Orders" (*Chumon no oi ryoriten*) and the first section of his well-known "Spring and Ashura" (*Haru to shura*). While neither of these was successful, they brought him to the attention of poets including Takamura Kotaro.

Miyazawa attempted to improve the material and the spiritual lives of peasants in the **impoverished** farming communities of Iwate. His poetry showed a great sensitivity to the land and the people who struggled to earn a living. A dedicated Buddhist, he sought to **renunciate** material values, serve others, and celebrate the natural world. His compassionate poetry and his life were aimed at helping those around him overcome poverty and misery. His best-known children's story is "Night on the Galactic Railroad" (*Ginga tetsudo no yoru*) and his best-known poem is probably "Unbeaten by the rain" (*Ame ni mo makezu*).

During his lifetime, his writing attracted little attention. But as the country began to rebuild after World War II, the sincerity of his spiritual struggle and sympathy with the impoverished attracted people who were trying to start new lives under harsh conditions. His works speak powerfully to progressive morals, contemporary sensibilities, and those who feel a deep connection with nature. (259)

宮沢賢治

自然をたたえ、人に奉仕

［1896-1933］

　宮沢賢治は岩手県の農村に生まれ、実家は仏教の信仰にあつい裕福な質屋だった。貧しい農民たちのなけなしの財産を質に入れさせて稼ぐ家業を継ぐことに抵抗を示し、宗教観をめぐる父親との軋轢から教師の道に進み、その後、執筆活動を行うようになった。

　童話『注文の多い料理屋』や、よく知られた詩集『春と修羅』を刊行。どちらもあまり売れなかったが、高村光太郎をはじめとする詩人らに認められるようになった。

　宮沢は、貧困にあえぐ岩手の農民たちの物質的・精神的生活の向上に努めた。宮沢の詩には、土地や、生計を立てるのに苦労している人々への強い思いが感じられる。熱心な仏教徒だった宮沢は、物質的価値観を捨て、人に奉仕し、自然をたたえようとした。情愛に満ちた詩と宮沢の人生は、周囲の人々が貧困や悲惨な生活を乗り越える支えになることを目指したものだった。最も有名な童話は『銀河鉄道の夜』、そして最も有名な詩はおそらく「雨ニモマケズ」だろう。

　生前はあまり注目を集めることはなかったが、日本が第2次世界大戦後の復興期を迎えると、宮沢の精神的に苦闘するひたむきさと貧困層への共感が、過酷な状況下で生活を立て直そうとする人々の心を捉えた。宮沢の作品には、進歩的な道徳観や現代的な感性、自然との深いつながりを感じる人々に力強く訴え掛けるものがある。

■prosperous 裕福な　■pious 信心深い　■meager 乏しい　■impoverished 貧窮化した　■renunciate 捨てる

84 Kato Shidzue
Campaigner for birth control and women's rights

Accompanying her first husband, a mining engineer, to his job at the Miike coal mine in Kyushu, Kato Shidzue **was appalled at** the conditions of the laborers. The men's working conditions in the mines was horrific. The women suffered from poverty and from **bearing** unwanted children, who died in large numbers.

When the couple traveled to the United States in 1919, Shidzue met the birth control **advocate** Margaret Sanger and was greatly moved. When Shidzue returned to Japan, she began to campaign for birth control, enabling women to plan their families responsibly. Shidzue later served as guide when Sanger visited Japan in 1922. Divorced from her husband, she supported her two sons by writing to promote social reform. Through this, she met and married the labor leader Kato Kanju.

Her efforts to limit the country's growing population faced **stiff resistance** in the 1930s from a militaristic regime that was fiercely hostile to limiting growth. On top of that, for a Japanese woman to **step out of** her traditional **submissive** role was considered a **breach** of morality. In the first elections following World War II, both she and Kato Kanju were elected to the House of Representatives, backed by the Japan Socialist Party. Subsequently she was elected to the **House of Councillors** in 1950 and served until 1974.

In two autobiographies, *Facing Two Ways* (which was translated into Japanese) and *Hitosuji no michi* (*A Straight Road*), she described her social views. She received the United Nations Population Award in 1988. (251)

加藤シヅエ

産児制限運動で女性の権利向上へ

［1897-2001］

　最初の結婚で、鉱山技師の夫の仕事に同行して九州の三池炭鉱を訪れた
加藤シヅエは、炭鉱労働者らが劣悪な環境で働いているのを見てショック
を受けた。男性の炭鉱での労働状況は悲惨なもので、女性は貧困と望まぬ
妊娠に苦しみ、亡くなる子どもも多かった。

　1919年に夫婦で渡米したシヅエは、産児制限運動の提唱者であるマーガ
レット・サンガーと出会い、感銘を受ける。帰国すると、産児制限運動を
始め、女性が責任を持って家族計画を立てられるように訴えた。1922年に
サンガーが来日した際には案内役を務めた。夫と離婚したシヅエは、社会
改革を推進する執筆活動を行いながら息子2人を養い、そうした活動の中
で労働運動家の加藤勘十と出会い、再婚する。

　シヅエの産児制限運動は、1930年代に「産めよ増やせよ」の政策を取る
軍国主義的な政権から反発を受けた。さらに、シヅエが昔からの従順な日
本人女性像という殻を打ち破ったことも道徳に反していると見なされた。
シヅエは第2次世界大戦後に行われた最初の総選挙で、日本社会党の後援
を受けて加藤勘十とともに当選し、衆議院議員（女性初）になる。その後、
1950年に参議院議員選挙で勝利し、1974年まで議員を務めた。

　自伝『Facing Two Way』（日本語の訳書は『ふたつの文化のはざまから』）
『ひとすじの道』では自身の社会観を語っている。1988年には国連人口賞
を受賞した。

■ be appalled at ～にショックを受ける　■ bear 出産する　■ advocate 提唱する
■ stiff resistance 激しい抵抗　■ step out of ～から降りる　■ submissive 従順な
■ breach 不履行　■ House of Councillors 参議院

85 Kawabata Yasunari
Japan the Beautiful

Kawabata Yasunari's childhood was filled with **misfortune**. Both of his parents died before he turned three years old. His sister and grandparents died by the time he was fourteen. This unhappy childhood is reflected in the melancholy and a sense of human **fragility** in his writings.

He entered Tokyo Imperial University in 1920 intending to major in English, but within a year he changed his major to Japanese literature. After graduation he **supported himself** through writing. He was **patronized** by important literary figures and began earning a modest living by writing literary reviews, participating in literary symposiums, and publishing short stories.

As a writer he seemed most **at home with** short stories. In fact, many of his novels, including *Thousand Cranes* (*Senbazuru*), were originally written as short stories. That novel was originally five separate stories, published in three different magazines, on five different occasions. His *Snow Country* (*Yukiguni*) was written and published in twelve segments between 1935 and 1947.

His works **progress** less through action than through a series of symbols, metaphors, and **allusions**. They are more like prose haiku than complex narratives with deep character **portrayals**. In fact, Kawabata **likened himself to** a **practitioner** of *renga*, linked verse. Nonetheless, his major works were translated into many European languages in the 1950s and 1960s.

Kawabata was awarded the Nobel Prize for Literature in 1968. In his acceptance speech, he **reconfirmed** his deep attachment to the beauty of the culture of his native land. (243)

川端康成

日本の美を描写し、世界へ

[1899-1972]

　川端康成は**不幸**な幼少期を送る。３歳になる前に両親が亡くなり、14歳になるまでに姉と祖父母もこの世を去った。不幸な生い立ちは、哀愁に満ちて人間のもろさを感じさせる川端の文章に反映されている。

　1920年、川端は東京帝国大学で英文科に入学するが、１年目で国文科に転向。卒業後は執筆を通じて**自活**した。著名な文学者らに**恩顧を受け**、書評の執筆、文学シンポジウムへの参加、短編小説の刊行などでそこそこの収入を得るようになった。

　作家として最も**得意**としていたと思われるのは短編小説で、川端の小説の多くは元は短編として書かれたものだった。その一つ『**千羽鶴**』は３誌で５回に分けて刊行された。『雪国』は1935〜1947年に12回に分載された。

　川端の作品は、（登場人物の）行動というよりむしろ象徴や**暗喩**、ほのめかしによって展開していく。人物**描写**を掘り下げた複雑な物語というよりは散文的な俳句に近く、実際、川端自身も**自身の作風**について**連歌**を**引き合いに出**している。そうした特徴の作品でありながら、主要な作品は1950年代から1960年代にかけて多くのヨーロッパ言語に翻訳された。

　川端は1968年にノーベル文学賞を受賞した。受賞した際の記念講演では、日本文化の美しさへの愛着を**再確認**したと述べている。

■ misfortune 不幸　　■ fragility もろさ　　■ supported oneself 自活する
■ patronize 後援する　■ at home with 〜に熟達している　■ progress 進展する
■ allusion さりげない言及　■ portrayal 描写　■ likened oneself to 自分を〜に
例える　■ practitioner 実践者　■ reconfirm 再確認する

86 Sugihara Chiune
Acts of Conscience

Sugihara Chiune entered the Foreign Ministry and **was posted to** the city of Harbin, where he spent 16 years, attaining **fluency** in Russian. He transferred from one post in Harbin to service in the diplomatic corps in Manchukuo, but when it became a **puppet state** of the Japanese military, in protest of the army's inhumane actions there, he resigned from this new position.

The Foreign Ministry eventually posted him to Lithuania. He arrived days before the German army invaded Poland. In July 1940, thousands of Jewish refugees, mostly from Poland, **lined up** outside the Japanese consulate hoping to obtain **transit visas** to escape Nazi capture and concentration camps. Transit visas were only issued to people with visas to another country after passing through Japan. Applicants had to prove that they had means to support themselves while in Japan, but many who came to the consulate had no such documents. His Tokyo superiors replied that he should not issue such visas because Germany was Japan's ally.

Nevertheless, Sugihara **put** his job **on the line** by signing visas on July 29. He continued all that day, and the next. He was still issuing visas on the morning of his departure for Japan in September. **Disobeying orders** from the Foreign Ministry, he signed over 2,000 visas for Jewish refugees and their dependents, saving more than 6,000 people from **extermination** by the Nazis.

Upon his return to Japan, he was relieved of his duties. After the war ended, he worked for a Japanese trading company and spent 15 years in Moscow. Only after his death did the Japanese government recognize his acts of **conscience** in saving the lives of so many Jewish refugees. (279)

杉原千畝

良心に従い多くの命を救った外交官

［1900-1986］

　杉原千畝は外務省の官費留学生としてハルビン（現・中国）に派遣され、ロシア語を修得。同省に採用されて、ハルビンで16年を過ごす。ハルビンから満州国外交部へ転任するが、日本の傀儡国家となった満州国での非人道的な軍の行為に嫌気がさして退官した。

　外務省から最終的に選ばれた赴任先はリトアニアだった。杉原がリトアニアに到着した数日後、ドイツ軍がポーランドに侵攻する。1940年7月、日本領事館の前には、ナチスに捕らえられて強制収容所送りになることから逃れようとするユダヤ人難民が、通過ビザを求めて大勢並んでいた。大半がポーランド出身者だった。通過ビザは、他国のビザを所持して日本を通過する人にしか発給されていなかった。申請が認められるには、日本滞在中に自活する手段があることを証明しなければならなかったが、領事館を訪れた多くの人はそうした書類を持っていなかった。東京の上司らは杉原に対し、ドイツは日本の同盟国であることからビザを出してはならないと指示する。

　だが杉原は7月29日、外務省から免職されるのを覚悟で、ビザ発給にサインした。その日ずっと、また翌日も、9月の帰国する日の朝でさえビザを発給し続けた。そうして杉原は外務省の指示に背き、ユダヤ人難民とその家族のために2,000（家族）以上のビザに署名し、6,000以上の人々をナチスのユダヤ人絶滅計画から救った。

　帰国後、杉原は（実質的に）免職された。終戦後は日本の商社に勤務し、モスクワで15年間過ごした。杉原が良心に従い、大勢のユダヤ人の命を救った行動が日本政府に認められたのは、死後になってからのことである。

■ be posted to ～に就けられる　■ fluency 流暢さ　■ puppet state 傀儡国家
■ line up 並ぶ　■ transit visas 通過ビザ　■ put ～ on the line ～を危険にさらす
■ disobey orders 命令に逆らう　■ extermination 絶滅　■ conscience 良心

87 Ozu Yasujiro
Cinematic Social Critic

At the age of ten, Ozu, his brothers, and his mother were sent to live in his father's hometown, while his father worked in Tokyo. Ozu spent much of his youth in movie theaters and in 1923 became an assistant cameraman with the Shochiku Company. Within four years, he was a **full-fledged** director.

After producing short comedies, he began producing movies about the modern Japanese family. In *Umareta wa mita keredo* (I Was Born but...) in 1932, he created the first great work of Japanese **cinematic social criticism**. There was a clear **parallel between** his personal life **and** his art in *Chichi ariki* (There Was a Father) in 1942, the story of a **subdued** but strong affection between a son and father that endured despite a long separation.

Ozu's masterpiece was *Tokyo monogatari* (Tokyo Story), a critical **depiction** of the negative impact of postwar society on the family. Toward the end of his film career, Ozu seemed to **become resigned to** the way the world was changing. His characters suffer disappointments, but with a degree of acceptance and faint humor.

The dialogue in Ozu's films **mimics** everyday conversation. The films are simple in essence, proceeding leisurely. There is a minimum of drama, but there is tension between the traditional and the modern that is the essence of most people's lives. While his films **are rooted in** a specifically Japanese atmosphere, they **convey** a universal hope for a family life that is secure, happy, and filled with affection. Ozu is perhaps the most Japanese of all the major directors. (258)

小津安二郎

映画で戦後社会を批評

［1903-1963］

　東京に生まれた小津安二郎（おづやすじろう）は10歳のときに、東京で働く父親だけを残して母親と兄弟と一緒に父の郷里（きょうり）（三重県松阪（まつざか））に移り住んだ。青春時代は多くの時間を映画館で過ごし、1923年に松竹の撮影助手の仕事に就き、4年後に監督として独り立（ひと）ちする。

　短い喜劇映画を制作した後、現代の日本の家族をテーマにした映画を撮り始めた。1932年の秀作『大人の見る繪本（えほん）　生れてはみたけれど』で、日本で初めて映画で社会批評を試みた。1942年の『父ありき』は、自身の私生活と明らかな共通点がある作品で、長い間離れて暮らしていた父と息子の心に秘めた強い情愛を描いている。

　代表作『東京物語』では、戦後社会が家族にもたらした悪影響を批判的に描いた。キャリアの終盤には、変化していく社会のあり方に対する諦念も感じさせ、小津映画の登場人物たちは失意の中でも、現実をある程度受け入れながら、そこはかとないユーモアを漂わせている。

　小津映画のセリフは日常的な会話を思わせ、作品は本質的にシンプルで、ゆっくりと展開していく。ドラマチックな要素は最小限に抑えられているものの、大半の人々の生活の根底にあるような伝統的な価値観と現代の価値観がぶつかり合う緊張感が張り詰めている。小津映画は日本的な（家族主義的）雰囲気に根ざし、家庭生活は幸福で愛情に満ち、揺るぎないものという普遍的な希望を伝えている。小津は、有名監督の中で最も日本人的な監督といえるかもしれない。

■full-fledged 一人前の　　■cinematic 映画の　　■social criticism 社会批判
■parallel … between 〜 …と〜の類似点　　■subdued 抑えられた　　■depiction
描写　　■become resigned to 〜を甘受するようになる　　■mimic 模倣する　　■be
rooted in 〜に根ざしている　　■convey 伝える

88 Munakata Shiko

Spontaneity and Passion for Art

Born in a poor family in Aomori Prefecture, Munakata received only an elementary school education. But he had artistic passion, and in 1924, **determined to** make painting his career, he moved to Tokyo. He **submitted an entry** in the annual Japan Art Academy exhibition four times without success. Finally in 1928, one of his paintings was accepted. But by that year, he was already shifting from oil painting to woodblock printing, becoming a student of Hiratsuka Un'ichi, a woodcut artist who focused on traditional Buddhist subjects in distinctively modern black-and-white prints.

In 1935 Yanagi Muneyoshi, founder of the folk art (*mingei*) movement, saw Munakata's works at an exhibition and purchased 25 prints. This changed Munakata's life. From then on, he visited temples and produced works with Buddhist religious imagery. *Ten Great Disciples of the Buddha* (1939) is **arguably** his masterpiece. He began with monochrome, but at Yanagi's suggestion, he began experimenting with color too.

During the **Tokyo air raids** of 1945, his house and most of his woodblocks were destroyed. After the war, he moved his studio to Kamakura, where he produced illustrated books, scrolls, watercolor paintings, and woodcuts **at a frenetic pace**. His bold, **rough-hewn** woodblock prints received international awards, and museums around the world collected his works.

His enormous **output incorporates** Japanese and Western influences, Buddhist images, Nebuta festival folk heroes, and Shinto deities. Rarely making preparatory sketches, he created his works with **spontaneity** and great energy, following, he said, what was inside the woodblock that he was carving. (251)

棟方志功

彫ることに情熱を捧げた版画家

［1903-1975］

　青森県の貧しい家庭に生まれた棟方志功は小学校卒業後、芸術にかける情熱から、1924年、画家を目指して上京。帝展（現・日展）に油絵を出品するが、4回落選した。1928年、ついに油絵が入選するが、この頃にはすでに棟方は平塚運一に師事し、油絵に代わって木版画を制作するようになっていた。平塚は、伝統的な仏教版画を題材に、非常にモダンな白黒版画で知られた版画家である。

　1935年、民芸運動の創始者、柳宗悦（p.170）が展覧会で棟方の作品を見て25枚の版画を購入したことで、棟方の人生は変わった。これ以後、棟方はさまざまな寺を訪ね、仏教的主題を表現した作品を制作していった。代表作は『二菩薩釈迦十大弟子』（1939年）である。最初は白黒だったが、柳の提案で色彩木版画にも挑戦するようになった。

　1945年の東京大空襲で自宅と版木のほとんどが焼失。戦後は鎌倉にアトリエを移し、絵本、巻物、水彩画、木版画などを驚異的なペースで制作。大胆で粗削りな木版画は国際的な賞を受賞し、世界中の美術館に作品が収集されるようになった。

　棟方の膨大な作品には、日本と欧米の影響や、仏やねぶたの題材となっている英雄、日本の神々などが取り入れられている。下絵はほとんど描かず、自身が「板木の中にあるものを彫っている」と述べた通り、内なる衝動に突き動かされながら、すさまじいエネルギーで作品を制作していった。

■determined to ～を決心して　■submit an entry 応募する　■arguably ほぼ
間違いなく　■Tokyo air raids 東京大空襲　■at a frenetic pace 猛烈な勢いで
■rough-hewn 粗削りの　■output 生産物　■incorporate ～を包含する
■spontaneity 自発性

89 Honda Soichiro
Nonconforming Revolutionary

Honda Soichiro's career began as a child when he helped his father, a bicycle dealer, repair bicycles. He left home in 1922 for Tokyo, where he became an **apprentice** in a garage, where he learned the basics of automobile engines. Following World War II, Honda, a highly innovative engineer, organized the Honda Motor company in 1948. He began in a wooden shack manufacturing motors for bicycles, producing the Type A **motorized** bicycle. With the Type D, he created a true motorcycle.

Honda revolutionized the motorcycle industry by developing a series of revolutionary new models with powerful engines. Building the largest motorcycle plant in the world in Mie Prefecture, he exported machines throughout the world. In 1961 his vehicles took first place in the international motorcycle race on the Isle of Man, making Honda the world's largest manufacturer.

As a **nonconformist**, Honda rejected the typical Japanese managerial traditions and instead promoted "the Honda Way," which was based on personal initiative and a close worker-management relationship. His refusal to conform **clashed with** the Japanese government's attempt to keep the country's auto industry limited to only a few powerful firms. His company began producing automobiles in 1963. Honda Motor entered the four-wheeled vehicle market with a series of innovations including a low-pollution CVCC engine.

Honda introduced the Civic to the American market in 1972. As a result of its remarkable **fuel efficiency**, it gained popularity beginning in the 1970s, even though small cars still appealed to a limited audience. Consecutive new designs and improvements helped Honda become Japan's third largest auto manufacturer by the early 1980s. (263)

本田宗一郎

伝統的な経営方法を否定した改革者

［1906-1991］

　本田宗一郎の経歴は、子どもの頃に自転車販売店の父の自転車修理を手
伝ったことから始まる。1922年に（地元の静岡から）上京し、自動車修理
工場で見習い（丁稚）として働き、自動車エンジンの基礎を学んだ。第2
次世界大戦後、革新的なエンジニアだった本田は、1948年に本田技研工業
を設立。木造バラックで自転車用補助エンジンの製造を始め、A型エンジ
ンを積んだ原動付自転車を生産。さらに、D型エンジンを搭載した本格的
なオートバイを造った。

　本田技研は、強力なエンジンを搭載した画期的な車種を次々と開発し、
二輪車業界に革命を起こした。三重県に世界最大の二輪車工場を建設し、
世界にオートバイを輸出。1961年にはイギリスのマン島で開催された国際
オートバイレースで優勝し、世界的な二輪車メーカーとなった。

　本田は型にはまらない人間で、日本の伝統的な経営方法を否定し、個人
の主体性と従業員を尊重したマネジメントに基づく「ホンダウェイ」を推
進した。同調をよしとしない本田の姿勢は、日本の自動車産業を一握りの
大手企業に限定しようとする政府の思惑とも対立したものの、本田技研は
1963年に四輪車の製造を開始し、低公害用CVCCエンジンをはじめとする
さまざまな技術革新で自動車市場に参入した。

　1972年に小型車シビックをアメリカ市場で発売。小型車は限られた層に
のみ好まれたが、それでも燃費の良さで1970年代に人気を博すようになっ
た。絶えず新たなデザインや改良を重ね続け、本田技研は1980年代初頭に
は国内第3位の自動車メーカーに成長した。

■apprentice 職人などの徒弟　■motorized 動力の付いた　■nonconformist 体
制などに従わない人　■clash with 〜と対立する　■fuel efficiency 燃費の良さ

90 Yukawa Hideki
Innovative Physics Research

Yukawa Hideki was the first Japanese to win a Nobel Prize, in any field. His **achievement** is impressive because he was educated in Japan, only going abroad after he made his first important discoveries. In addition, his research was **carried on** partly under wartime conditions. It is said that parts of his discovery came from giving free rein to his imagination on nights when he could not sleep.

He studied in Kyoto, became a lecturer at Osaka University, and then became a professor at Kyoto University in 1939. He remained there during World War II.

While atomic physicists knew that the nucleus contained both protons and neutrons, no one knew what held the two **nuclear particles** together. Yukawa was the first to suggest that they were bound together by another particle, which he called a "meson." He discovered that only one kind, the **pi meson** or **pion**, carried the force that could **mediate** the nuclear force. This pi meson was produced for the first time in 1948.

In 1948, he was invited to join other world-class researchers including Robert Oppenheimer for a year at the Institute of Advanced Study at Princeton. In 1949 Yukawa became professor of physics at Columbia University and he received the Nobel for Physics for his work on mesons. He gave up this honored position at Columbia in 1953 to become director of Kyoto University's Research Institute for Fundamental Physics. While serving in many high-level government and educational posts, he remained a **vocal** advocate for the peaceful use of atomic energy. (255)

湯川秀樹

革新的な世界的物理学者
［1907-1981］

　湯川秀樹は、日本人として初めてノーベル賞を受賞した。湯川のすごいところは、日本国内で教育を受け、海外に行ったのは、初めて重要な発見を成し遂げた後だったことだ。研究の一部も戦時下で行い、眠れない夜に自由に想像を働かせたことが発見につながったとされている。

　京都帝国大学（物理学科）で学んだ後、大阪帝国大学講師となり、1939年に京都帝国大学教授となった。第2次世界大戦中も京都にとどまった。

　原子物理学の世界では、原子核に陽子と中性子が含まれていることは知られていたが、この2つの核の粒子がどうやって結合しているかは分かっていなかった。湯川は初めて、陽子と中性子はもう一つの粒子、中間子によって結合しているという考えを展開。核力を媒介することができるのは、π（パイ）中間子と呼ばれる粒子のみであることを発見した。このπ中間子は1948年に初めて人工的に生成された。

　同年1948年には、オッペンハイマーら世界的な研究者たちに招かれ、プリンストン高等研究所で1年間、客員教授を務めた。1949年、コロンビア大学の物理学部の客員教授に就任、同年中間子理論の研究でノーベル物理学賞を受賞した。1953年に退任し、京都大学基礎物理学研究所の所長に就任した。さまざまな行政機関や教育機関の要職に就く一方で、原子力の平和利用を声をあげて訴え続けた。

■achievement 業績　■carry on 行う　■nuclear particle 核子　■pi meson
パイ中間子　■pion パイオン、パイ中間子　■mediate 媒介となる　■vocal 声高
な

91 Kurosawa Akira
Human Complexity

Initially seeking a career as a painter, Kurosawa instead became an assistant director at what became Toho Co., Ltd. After developing his scriptwriting skills, he directed his first film in 1943, the story of a young **practitioner** of judo titled *Sugata Sanshiro*. The success of the film established his reputation as a director.

It was a story set in medieval Japan that brought him international recognition. Based on two stories by Akutagawa Ryunosuke, *Rashomon* presented a murder case, in which four parties, including the victim and his murderer, present their perspectives of the crime. This superb **portrayal** of human **subjectivity** in shaping "the truth" won Kurosawa the first Japanese grand prize at the 1951 Venice Film Festival.

Films like "The Idiot" (*Hakuchi*, 1951) and "To Live" (*Ikiru*, 1952) showed Kurosawa's concern with the question of how a person ought to live. They are serious films, showing the director's **philosophical** side.

Shichinin no samurai (Seven Samurai) in 1954 presented exciting battle scenes, but did so with considerable moral insight. With the possible exception of *Rashomon*, it is possibly his best known film, and one of the best known Japanese films in the West.

When his films turned into **big-budget** spectacles, his career seemed **at risk**. With support from Francis Ford Coppola and Steven Spielberg, however, he was able to produce "The Shadow Warrior" (*Kagemusha*, 1980) and *Ran* (1985), epic films about the horrors that are **unleashed** by the lust for power. Kurosawa's films were never just dramatic spectacles or exhibitions of violence. They inevitably **dealt with** the **motivations**, darkness, and **complexity** of humanity. (262)

黒澤明

人間の複雑さを描いた映画監督

[1910-1998]

　黒澤明は最初は画家志望だったが、現在の東宝で助監督となり、脚本の腕を磨いた後、1943年、若き柔道家を主人公にした『姿三四郎』で監督デビューする。同作の成功により、監督として一躍評判を得た。

　中世の日本を舞台にした『羅生門』では国際的な評価を得る。芥川龍之介（p.172）の2編の短編小説を翻案した同作は、被害者と下手人を含む当事者4者の視点で殺人事件を描いている。人の主観が「真実」を形作っていく様を見事に描き出し、1951年のヴェネチア国際映画祭で日本人初の金獅子賞（グランプリ）を受賞した。

　1951年の『白痴』や1952年の『生きる』は、人はどう生きるべきかという問題に対する黒澤の関心を示しており、いずれも黒澤の哲学的な一面が表れたシリアスな作品だ。

　1954年の『七人の侍』は、エキサイティングな戦闘シーンが描かれている一方で、深い道徳的洞察力も兼ね備えている。おそらく『羅生門』を除けば、黒澤作品として最も有名な映画で、海外でも最も認知度の高い日本映画の1本だ。

　巨額の予算を投じた大作を撮るようになるにつれ、黒澤のキャリアにも陰りが見えたように思えたが、フランシス・フォード・コッポラやスティーヴン・スピルバーグの働きかけで、1980年の『影武者』や1985年の『乱』など、権勢欲が爆発したときの恐怖を描いた叙事詩的な映画を制作することができた。黒澤の映画は、単にドラマチックな大作やバイオレンスを売り物とするようなものではなく、必ず人の欲求や闇、複雑さを描いている。

■ practitioner 実践家　　■ portrayal 描写　　■ subjectivity 主観性
■ philosophical 哲学の　■ big-budget 多額の予算を投じた　■ at risk 危険にさらされて　■ unleash 爆発させる　■ deal with 〜を取り上げる　■ motivation（行動の）動機付け　■complexity 複雑さ

92 Okamoto Taro
Outside the Box

Okamoto Taro went to France with his parents in 1929. He studied art in Paris for a decade and associated with major figures of Surrealism, including Andre Breton and Kurt Seligmann, and with abstract artists, including Picasso, Man Ray, and Robert Capa.

Following the German **invasion** of France, in 1940 he returned to Japan and military duty in China. When he returned to Tokyo after the war, he found that all of his stored drawings and paintings had burned during the bombings. His reaction was to simply start over again.

A **prolific** writer, he published *Mysteries in Japan* (*Shinpi Nihon*) in 1964. It was sparked by an interest in Jomon pottery and he travelled around Japan researching what he considered to be mysterious elements **underlying** Japanese culture.

As an artist, Okamoto believed that art should be shared and he created many large pieces of public art. His most famous work is *Tower of the Sun*, which became the centerpiece of the 1970 World Expo in Osaka. The lower part **represents** the past, the middle part stands for the present, and the face portrays the future of the human race.

A second striking work is his **mural** *Tomorrow's Mythology* (*Asu no shinwa*) which was originally created for a Mexican hotel but now stands in Shibuya Station. Depicting a human figure struck by an atomic bomb, rather than pure **lament**, it conveys an acceptance of what happened, yet **embraces** future change with a sense of wonderment. (244)

岡本太郎

既存の枠に収まらない芸術家

［1911-1996］

　1929年、両親と渡仏した岡本太郎（おかもと たろう）は、パリで10年間美術を学び、シュルレアリスムの大家、アンドレ・ブルトンやクルト・セリグマン、抽象画家のピカソやマン・レイ、ロバート・キャパらと交流した。

　ドイツ軍のフランス**侵攻**を機に1940年に帰国し、中国に出征（しゅっせい）。終戦後、復員して東京に戻ってくると、保管していたドローイングや絵画は空襲ですべて焼失していた。岡本の反応は、ただ一からやり直そうというものであった。

　多作の岡本は、1964年には『神秘日本』を出版。縄文（じょうもん）土器に触発され、国内各地を巡り、日本文化の**根底にある**と考えた神秘的な要素について洞（どう）察（さつ）を深めた。

　芸術家としての岡本は、芸術は（芸術家や美術愛好家たちだけのものでなく）共有するべきものだとの信念から、パブリックアートの大作を数多く制作。最も有名な作品は、1970年の大阪万博の中心的な作品となった『太陽の塔』である。この作品の下部は人類の過去、中部は現在、顔は未来を**表して**いる。

　次に印象的な作品は、**壁画**『明日の神話』だ。メキシコのホテルに依頼されて岡本が制作したこの作品は、現在、渋谷駅に設置されている。描かれているのは（アメリカの水爆実験で）被爆（ひばく）した人間の姿だが、ただ**嘆き**悲しんでいるというよりは、起こった事実を**受け入れ**、戸惑いながらも、未来を切り開いていく気持ちが表現されている。

■ invasion 侵攻　■ prolific 多作の　■ underlying 下にある　■ represent 表す
■ mural 壁画　■ lament 嘆き　■ embrace 受け入れる

93 Tange Kenzo
Architectural Freedom

Firebombing during World War II reduced major portions of Japan's urban areas to **rubble**. Following this destruction came a historic **burst** of reconstruction. It was an extraordinary opportunity for a young, **enterprising** architect to define the **literal** shape of postwar Japan. A graduate of the University of Tokyo, Tange Kenzo quickly established himself as a major architect.

As an internationally known architect and city planner, Tange is known for buildings that are boldly shaped and urban complexes that are functional, not dependent on **rigid geometric** framework. Among his technological innovations in architecture is the "shell structure." More than anything, he is recognized for blending traditional Japanese aesthetics with modern expression.

Tange's more dramatic works include the design for the Hiroshima Peace Memorial Park. The museum that houses information about the explosion is in the center of the park, and is raised on **piloti**. The concept of plain concrete surfaces was to avoid **distracting** from the exhibits inside. His iconic Yoyogi National Stadium for the 1964 Tokyo Olympics was inspired by the Roman Colosseum and by Le Corbusier. He took Western ideas, adapted them to Japanese requirements, and created the world's largest **suspended** roof span. Among other major projects he carried out are the theme pavilion for Expo '70 in Osaka, the massive Tokyo Metropolitan Government Offices in 1991, and the Fuji TV Building in 1996.

Tange also taught at various universities and among his students were Maki Fumihiko, Isozaki Arata, and Kurokawa Kisho. He inspired whole generations of architects as well, both in Japan and abroad. (256)

丹下健三

自由に発想した建築家

［1913-2005］

　日本の都市部は、第2次世界大戦中の空襲により、その大部分が瓦礫（がれき）と化し、破壊を経て歴史的な復興ラッシュが始まった。若くて進取の気性に富んだ建築家にとっては、戦後日本を文字通り一から造っていく絶好の機会となり、東京大学を卒業した丹下健三（たんげけんぞう）は、たちまち頭角を現し、主要な建築家としての地位を確立した。

　世界的に有名な建築家で都市設計家の丹下は、大胆な形をした建物や機能的な複合施設などで知られ、幾何学的で硬直した枠組みにとらわれなかった。建築に対する丹下の技術革新の一つが（曲面を利用した）「シェル構造」だ。丹下が何より評価されているのは、日本の伝統的な美意識と現代的な表現方法を融合させたことにある。

　丹下が設計を手掛けた印象的な作品としては、広島平和記念公園がある。公園の中央にあるのは、原爆についての資料を展示したピロティ（2階を1階の柱で支えた建築）様式の広島平和会館原爆記念陳列館（現・広島平和記念資料館）。打ちっ放しのコンクリートは、人々に展示物に集中してもらうことを狙っていた。1964年の東京五輪会場で丹下の代表作となった国立代々木競技場は、ローマのコロッセオやル・コルビュジエに着想を得たものだった。丹下は欧米のアイデアを取り入れながら、日本での条件に合わせ、世界最大のスパン構造の吊（つ）り屋根を生み出した。これ以外の重要な事業として、1970年の大阪万博の中心施設となるパビリオン（お祭り広場）、1991年の巨大な東京都庁、1996年のフジテレビ（本社）ビルなどの設計がある。

　丹下はさまざまな大学で教壇に立ち、教え子には槇文彦（まきふみひこ）、磯崎新（いそざきあらた）、黒川紀章（くろかわきしょう）らがおり、国内外のあらゆる世代の建築家に影響を与えた。

■ rubble がれき　■ burst 突発　■ enterprising 進取的な　■ literal 文字通りの
■ rigid 柔軟性に欠ける　■ geometric 幾何学的な　■ piloti ピロティ（建物を持ち上げ地表を開放する様式の支柱）　■ distract （人の気を）そらす　■ suspend 吊るす

94 Tanaka Kakuei
The Builder

With only an elementary school education, Tanaka Kakuei established a construction company as a young man and **earned a fortune** during World War II, enabling him to make substantial contributions to a postwar political party. That **eased** his entry into politics, and he was elected to the House of Representatives in 1947. He became a member of the Liberal Democratic Party when it was established in 1955.

Serving as minister of postal services and telecommunications, then as minister of finance, Tanaka became prime minister in 1972. He advocated an economic plan based on *Nihon retto kaizo ron*, Plan for Remodeling the Japanese **Archipelago**, a book he published just before taking office. The goal of this proposal was to **deconcentrate** industry from the heavily populated and polluted Tokyo-Osaka industrial belt. To do this, he planned to form regional industrial centers and planned to link them with **superhighways** and high-speed shinkansen trains. Opponents saw that as spreading pollution, weakening farming communities, and reducing **agricultural self-sufficiency**.

In the end, the plan sent inflation and real estate speculation into **overdrive**. When the oil crisis of 1973 came, the plan was **abandoned**.

He resigned from the government in 1974, and was arrested in 1976 in connection with a scandal involving the Lockheed Aircraft Corporation. He **was indicted** and sentenced to prison, but continued to exercise power as the "Shadow Shogun" while **appealing his sentence**. Despite his **ignominious** end, his image as a **self-made** man, his attempt to improve the lives of the people, and reestablishment of relations with China made him a charismatic political figure. (259)

田中角栄

たたき上げのカリスマ政治家

［1918-1993］

　小学校教育しか受けていない田中角栄（たなかかくえい）は、若くして建設会社を立ち上げ、第2次世界大戦中に**財を成して**、戦後の政党に多額の献金をする。それが縁で政界入りし、1947年に衆議院議員に当選。1955年に結成された自由民主党の一員となった。

　郵政相、通産相、大蔵相などを経て、1972年に首相に就任。直前に出版した『日本列島改造論』で主張した経済計画を推進した。目的は、人口が集中し、公害汚染の多い東京・大阪の工業地帯から産業を地方に分散させることにあった。そのために田中は、地方に産業センターを形成し、**高速道路**や新幹線でつなげることを計画した。反対派は、公害が広がる中で農村社会が弱体化し、**食料自給率**が低下すると主張した。

　最終的に田中の政策はインフレと不動産投機の**加熱**を招き、1973年のオイルショックで**頓挫**（とんざ）した。

　1974年に田中は退陣。1976年には航空機製造大手ロッキード社の**不祥事**（ふしょうじ）への関与で逮捕・**起訴**されて実刑判決を受けたが、**控訴**中も「闇将軍」として影響力を行使し続けた。**不名誉な晩年**を迎えたが、たたき上げのイメージと国民生活の向上を図った政策、日中国交正常化により、政治家としてカリスマ的な存在になった。

■ earn a fortune 財を成す　　■ ease 容易にする　　■ archipelago 列島
■ deconcentrate 分散する　■ superhighway 高速道路　■ agricultural self-sufficiency 農業の自給自足　■ overdrive 加熱　■ abandon 放棄する　■ be indicted 起訴される　■ appeal one's sentence 控訴する　■ ignominious 恥ずべき　■ self-made 自力で出世した

95 Saruhashi Katsuko

Science Trailblazer

Saruhashi Katsuko gave up her first job to enter Toho University and received a degree in physics in 1943. She joined the **forerunner** of the Japan Meteorological Agency, where she studied oceans. She developed the first method for measuring CO_2 using temperature, pH, and chlorinity, called Saruhashi's Table, which became the global standard.

Saruhashi led the way in studying **nuclear contamination** in the ocean. When Japanese fishermen became seriously ill after the United States carried out nuclear tests near Bikini Atoll, the Japanese government sent her and fellow researchers to investigate. They found that ocean currents pushed radiation-contaminated water clockwise in the Pacific, and it took just 18 months for radioactivity to reach Japan. This research provided the evidence necessary to bring the U.S., UK and the Soviet Union to an agreement to end **above-ground** nuclear testing in 1963.

At various research institutes, she **contended with** various types of **prejudice.** Overcoming this, she left a **lasting** impression in her field, due to her deep belief that scientists bear social responsibility. She engaged with the public, taught them about her work, and listened to their opinions regarding what scientists should **prioritize.**

The first woman to earn a PhD in chemistry at the University of Tokyo in 1957, she was elected to the Science Council of Japan, won prizes in **geochemistry**, and promoted the peaceful use of nuclear power. She also founded the Society of Japanese Women Scientists as a forum for solving problems facing women scientists. In 1981 she founded the Saruhashi Prize, a **prestigious** award given to Japanese women scientists. (260)

猿橋勝子

地球科学を切り開いた先駆者

［1920-2007］

　猿橋勝子は就職するのをやめて帝国女子理学専門学校（現・東邦大学理学部）に入学し、1943年に物理学の学位を取得した。（女性研究者の）**先駆け**として気象庁の前身である中央気象台に入所し、海洋について研究。（海水中の）温度、pH（ペーハー）、塩素量を用いて炭酸物質量を測定する方法を考え出し、その方法は「サルハシの表」と呼ばれ、世界標準となった。

　猿橋は、海洋の**放射能汚染**の研究でも先駆者となった。アメリカがビキニ環礁で水爆実験を行った後、日本人の漁師らが重症化したことをきっかけに、日本政府は猿橋ら研究者を派遣して調査に乗り出した。その結果、放射能で汚染された海水が海流によって太平洋で時計回りに押し上げられ、放射性物質がわずか1年半で日本に到達していたことを突き止めた。この研究が実証となり、1963年に米英ソ間で**地下を除く空間**で核実験を禁止する部分的核実験禁止条約の成立につながった。

　猿橋はさまざまな研究機関で**偏見**を乗り越え、「科学者には社会的責任がある」という強い信念で、自身の研究分野に**永続的**な影響を与えた。また、科学者は何を**優先**するべきかという点で世間とのつながりを大事にし、自身の仕事について講演し、一般人の意見にも耳を傾けた。

　また、1957年には女性として初めて、東京大学で理学博士号を取得。日本学術会議会員に選出され、**地球化学**の分野（海洋化学）で賞を受賞し、原子力の平和利用を推進した。さらに、女性科学者が直面する問題を解決する場として日本女性科学者の会を設立。1981年には、日本人の女性科学者をたたえる「猿橋賞」を創設した。

■ forerunner 先駆者　■ nuclear contamination 放射能汚染　■ above-ground 地上の　■ contend with と闘う　■ prejudice 偏見　■ lasting 持続的な　■ prioritize 優先する　■ geochemistry 地球化学　■ prestigious 名誉ある

96 Morita Akio
Made in Japan as a Compliment

Together with chief **founder** Ibuka Masaru, Morita Akio established a company manufacturing radios and other electrical **gadgets** called Tokyo Tsushin Kogyo in 1946. The name was later changed to Sony Corporation, a name that would be easier for people abroad to remember.

Ibuka handled the research and development side; Morita handled the business side and worldwide marketing. In 1950 they marketed the first tape recorders produced in Japan, with great success. Then Ibuka **acquired** the **patent rights** for transistors from America's Western Electric Company and began developing transistor radios. Their **breakthrough** product was the world's smallest transistor radio, introduced on the world market in 1957.

Sony then began designing small-sized color televisions and videocassette recorders and players. At Morita's **insistence**, Sony manufactured the Sony Walkman portable tape player, an international hit among consumer electronics in the 1980s and 1990s.

To make Sony seem more "American," Morita led the establishing of a plant in San Diego and set up an importing business, Sony Trading Corporation. A **high point** for Sony came in 1970, when Morita had the company's stock **listed on** the New York Stock Exchange. Sony was the first Japanese stock to achieve that status. Before long, many people in the U.S. and other countries thought Sony was an American company.

In his later years, Morita became a major figure in Japanese business and in international **business circles** as well, as shown in his autobiography *Made in Japan: Akio Morita and Sony*, which was published in 1986. (247)

盛田昭夫

メイド・イン・ジャパンを世界中に

［1921-1999］

　盛田昭夫は1946年、井深大とともにラジオなどの電気機器を製造する東京通信工業株式会社を設立。その後、海外でも覚えてもらいやすいように、ソニーと社名を変更した。

　井深が研究開発、盛田が経営と世界的なマーケティングを担当し、1950年には日本初のテープレコーダーを発売し、大ヒットさせる。その後、井深はアメリカのウェスタン・エレクトリック社からトランジスタの特許を取得し、トランジスタラジオの開発に乗り出した。1957年には世界最小の画期的なトランジスタラジオを開発し、世界に売り込んだ。

　ソニーはその後、小型のカラーテレビやビデオカセットレコーダー、プレーヤーの開発にも着手し、盛田の主張で、1980年代から1990年代にかけて、世界的なヒット商品となった携帯カセットテーププレーヤー「ウォークマン」を製造した。

　ソニーを「アメリカナイズ」するため、盛田が中心となってサンディエゴに工場を設立し、輸入事業を手掛けるソニー・トレーディング・コーポレーションを設立。極め付けに、1970年、ソニーは日本企業として初めてニューヨーク証券取引所に上場した。やがて、アメリカをはじめとする国々で多くの人からソニーはアメリカ企業と見なされるようになった。

　晩年の盛田は、1986年に出版された自伝『MADE IN JAPAN─わが体験的国際戦略』でも紹介されているように、日本のみならず世界の経済界で重要人物となった。

■founder 創設者　■gadget 装置　■acquire 獲得する　■patent right 特許権
■breakthrough 画期的な　■insistence 主張　■high point 見せ場　■list on
〜に上場する　■business circle 経済界

97 Shiba Ryotaro
Traveling through History

After graduating from Osaka University of Foreign Studies, where he studied Mongolian, Shiba Ryotaro worked as a newspaper journalist, while writing in his spare time. His *Kaido o Yuku* series about his travels within Japan for the weekly magazine *Shukan Asahi* **lasted from** 1971 **to** 1996.

As a novelist, his **forte** was popular historical works, and he received the Naoki Prize for *Fukuro no shiro* (Castle of Owls) in 1960. Taking the **turbulent** period from the late Edo to early Meiji periods as his subject matter, he produced entirely new **interpretations** of the actions of the people involved.

His best-selling work, *Ryoma ga yuku* (1963-1966), is a historical novel about the samurai Sakamoto Ryoma, who was **instrumental** in bringing about the Meiji Restoration and transforming the country from feudal military rule in the 1860s. Beginning as a partisan who sought to restore the emperor to political power, Sakamoto came to realize that Japan needed to gain the technology and advanced industry that supported the Western powers.

Among Shiba's works translated into English is *Kukai no fukei, Kukai the Universal*, a **fictionalized biography** of the priest who founded the Shingon school of Buddhism in Japan. His multi-volume *Saka no ue no kumo* (1969-1972), translated into English as *Clouds above the Hill*, is a historical tale of the Akiyama brothers who devoted their energies during the Meiji period to building a modern Japanese military capability.

Many of Shiba's popular works led to TV **dramatizations**, most notably the year-long *taiga* dramas broadcast by NHK. (251)

司馬遼太郎

歴史大衆小説の大家
［1923-1996］

　司馬遼太郎は大阪外国語大学モンゴル語科を卒業した後、新聞記者として働くかたわら執筆活動を行った。1971年から1996年まで週刊誌「週刊朝日」で日本国内の紀行文「街道をゆく」シリーズを連載した。

　小説家としては、大衆的な歴史小説を**得意**とし、1960年に『梟の城』で直木賞を受賞。さらに幕末から明治初期の**激動**の時代を題材に、その当時の人々の行動を斬新な**解釈**で描いた。

　ベストセラーとなった『竜馬がゆく』（1963〜1966）は、1860年代に明治維新を実現させ、幕府が統治する封建的な時代を終わらせるのに**貢献**した坂本龍馬（p.110）を描いた歴史小説である。龍馬は、初めは尊王攘夷派だったが、日本には欧米列強を支えていた技術力と高度な産業を確立する必要があると気付くようになった幕末の志士である。

　司馬の作品で英訳されたものには、日本の真言宗の開祖、空海（p.24）の伝記小説『空海の風景』がある。長編『坂の上の雲』（1969〜1972）は、明治時代に日本の軍事力の近代化に尽力した秋山兄弟を題材にした歴史小説だ。

　司馬の人気作品の多くは**テレビドラマ化**され、とりわけNHKで１年通じて放映される大河ドラマが有名である。

■ last from … to〜 …から〜に続く　■ forte 強み　■ turbulent 不穏な
■ interpretation 解釈　■ instrumental 助けになる　■ fictionalized biography
伝記小説　■ dramatization ドラマ化

98 Mishima Yukio
Brilliant Competence

Mishima Yukio's most striking qualities as a writer may have been his **familiarity** with both Japanese and European literary traditions. As a writer, he **was competent in** simple and complex narratives; historical, philosophical, and lyrical works; as well as kabuki and noh plays.

His *Confessions of a Mask* (*Kamen no kokuhaku*) is semi-autobiographical. *After the Banquet* (*Utage no ato*) is an imaginative use of historical material about money and postwar politics. His *Sound of Waves* (*Shiosai*) is a **reworking** of an ancient Greek legend of Daphnis and Cloe. Mishima **is celebrated for** *The Temple of the Golden Pavilion* (*Kinkakuji, 1956*), based on the story of a nihilistic Buddhist **acolyte** who, in 1950, burned down the Kinkakuji. The acolyte is obsessed with his own **inadequacy** and sees the temple's perfect beauty as a reminder of his own imperfection. In a **desperate** act of **defiance** and self-liberation, he sets fire to the temple. In this novel, Mishima focuses on the contrasts of love and hate, reality and illusion, selflessness and **self-assertion**.

In the 1960s, Mishima began **addressing himself to** the student movement and the apparent lack of **mooring** in the postwar generation. Feeling that Japanese constantly adopted the new and then regretted the passing of tradition, he began to idealize traditional values, including idealizing the emperor system. Determined to act on his **convictions** and not die of old age, he chose death as a positive action. After failing to arouse the members of the Self-Defense Force to follow his philosophy, he committed seppuku, following the tradition of the samurai. (257)

三島由紀夫

才気煥発の小説家

[1925-1970]

　三島由紀夫の作家としての特筆すべき点は、日本と欧州の文学の伝統に**精通**していたことかもしれない。シンプルな話でも複雑な話でも**自在に扱**い、歴史物や哲学的な作品、叙情的な作品を手掛け、歌舞伎や能も創作した。

　『仮面の告白』は半自伝的な作品である。『宴のあと』はお金と戦後政治をめぐる実話を想像力豊かに描いた小説で、『潮騒』は古代ギリシャのダフニスとクロエの伝説に**ヒントを得た**小説である。『金閣寺』は三島が大きく**称賛**された作品で、1950年に金閣寺に放火した厭世的な僧をモデルにしている。主人公の**学僧**は、自分の**コンプレックス**に拘泥し、金閣寺の完璧な美しさのせいで自分の不完全さが思い知らされると考え、**自暴自棄**になり、自己を解放するために金閣寺に火をつける。三島はこの小説の中で、愛と憎しみ、現実と幻想、無私と**自己主張**のコントラストに焦点を当てている。

　三島は1960年代に入ると、学生運動や、戦後世代が**精神的なよりどころ**を明らかに失っていることに**向き合うようになる**。日本人は常に新しいものを取り入れては伝統が失われることを後悔しているのではないかと考え、天皇制を理想とするなど伝統的な価値観を理想化するようになった。自身の**信念**に従い、老いる前に死ぬと決意し、積極的な行動として死を選ぶ。自身の哲学に追随するよう自衛隊員に決起を促したがかなわず、武士の伝統に倣って**割腹自殺**した。

■familiarity 精通　■be competent in ～に優れている　■rework 改訂する
■be celebrate for ～で称賛する　■acolyte 侍者　■inadequacy 不十分
■desperate 捨てばちの　■defiance 抵抗　■self-assertion 誇示　■address
oneself to ～に専念する　■mooring 精神的なよりどころ　■conviction 信念

99 Ogata Sadako

Direct Humanitarian

Ogata Sadako was related to a prime minister and her father was Japanese ambassador to Finland. She spent her early years abroad, before graduating from the University of Sacred Heart in Tokyo. She did graduate work at Georgetown University and received her Ph.D. from the University of California, Berkeley, before becoming a professor at Sophia University.

In 1968, she was included in the Japanese delegation to the UN General Assembly. After holding several positions within the UN, Ogata took over the United Nations High Commissioner for Refugees (UNHCR) in 1991. She was the first female head of the refugee agency, a Japanese, and an **academic** in an organization that was crowded with former politicians and bureaucrats. Many doubted whether she **was up to** the challenges of running one of the world's largest humanitarian organizations. They quickly discovered that she was **decisive**, **pragmatic**, and highly capable.

Within weeks she was in the mountains of Iraq dealing **first-hand** with Kurds escaping from the Gulf War. She asked questions, listened to different sides, and sought their cooperation. Her chief of staff commented, "She understood immediately she had to **get off the pedestal** and into the battle." She moved the UNHCR into Cambodia, the Balkans, and Rwanda. One of the biggest changes she **implemented** was to help not only refugees crossing borders, but also internally displaced persons (IDPs).

She returned to Japan, and from 2003 to 2012 she headed the Japan International Cooperation Agency. She became a frequent critic of the Japanese government for failing to provide sanctuary to refugees from Syria and other conflicts. (261)

緒方貞子

現場で活動する人道主義者

［1927-2019］

　緒方貞子は、首相と親戚関係にあり（曽祖父が犬養毅）、父親はフィンランド特命全権公使だった。幼少期を海外で過ごし、東京の聖心女子大学を卒業。アメリカのジョージタウン大学を卒業し、カリフォルニア大学バークリー校で博士号を取得し、（のちに）上智大学教授に就任する。

　1968年、国連日本政府代表顧問を務め、国連でさまざまな役職を経て、1991年に国連難民高等弁務官（UNHCR）に就任。UNHCは政治家や官僚経験者が多い組織で、緒方は女性としても日本人としても**学者**としても初のトップだった。多くの人からは、世界最大級の人道組織を運営できるか疑問視されたが、緒方が**決断力に優れ**、**実際的**で、非常に有能であることはすぐに衆目の一致するところとなった。

　就任後数週間のうちに、イラクの山中で、湾岸戦争から避難してきたクルド難民に**直接**対応。質問し、さまざまな立場の人々の話に耳を傾け、協力を求めた。緒方の職務を補佐した職員は、「彼女は**上の立場から降りて**現場（の戦闘）に足を運ぶ必要性をただちに理解していた」と評している。緒方はUNHCRにカンボジア、バルカン半島、ルワンダを支援させた。緒方が**導入した**UNHCR最大の方向転換は、UNHCRの支援対象に国境を越えた難民だけではなく、国内避難民（国境を越えない避難民）も加えたことだ。

　帰国後、2003年から2012年まで国際協力機構（JICA）理事長に就任。緒方は、日本政府がシリアなどの紛争地域からの難民を受け入れないことについて繰り返し批判した。

■academic 学者　■be up to（任務など）を遂行できる　■decisive 決断力のある　■pragmatic 実際的な　■first-hand じかに　■get off the pedestal 尊敬されている立場から降りる　■implement 実行する

100 Tezuka Osamu
Master of Manga

Tezuka Osamu graduated from Osaka University Medical School and received an **M.D.** degree. But his career path **had little to do with** medicine.

While he was still a student in university, in 1946 he made his debut as a newspaper comic-strip artist. He was stimulated by Tagawa Suiho's children's **comic strip** *Norakuro* (Blackie the Stray), which ran in the *Shonen kurabu* (Boys' Club) magazine in the 1930s, and by Walt Disney. Tezuka's innovations included comic-strip novels and comic-strip science fiction. Highly **prolific** as an artist, he created a wide range of comics for both young people and for adult readers as well. He became a pioneer in the creation of visual stories.

Among his best-known series are *Janguru taitei* (*Kimba the White Lion*) and *Tetsuwan Atomu* (*Astro Boy*). From 1954 to 1988 he produced a series titled *Hi no tori* (*Phoenix 2772*). This **long-running** series dealt with serious issues in human life in a comic-strip form which **broke new ground** in the field. It was, according to Tezuka, his lifework. Tezuka went on to making animated versions of his comics for both movies and television.

Prolific and innovative, Tezuka came to be regarded as "the father of manga". At least part of his legacy is his belief that manga could be a means of **convincing** people **to** care for the world. (221)

手塚治虫

漫画の父にして神様

［1928-1989］

　手塚治虫は大阪大学医学専門部を卒業し、**医学博士号**を取得するが、その後、医学とはほとんど関係のない世界に進む。

　大学在学中の1946年に新聞の4コマ漫画の連載でデビュー。影響を受けたのは、1930年代に「少年倶楽部」誌に掲載されていた田河水泡の漫画『のらくろ』やウォルト・ディズニーの漫画だった。手塚は、連載物の**漫画**小説やSFなど、革新的な作品を発表。**多作**で知られ、若者向けから大人向けまで、幅広いジャンルの漫画を手掛け、ストーリー漫画の先駆者となった。

　代表作は『ジャングル大帝』『鉄腕アトム』など。1954年から1988年にかけては『火の鳥』を制作した。このシリーズ**長編**ものは、人の一生におけるシリアスな問題を漫画で表現したもので、この分野の**新境地を切り開**いた。手塚によれば、ライフワークといえる作品だ。手塚はその後も、映画やテレビ向けに自身の漫画をアニメ化し、活動を続けた。

　精力的で革新的な手塚は「漫画の父」と見なされる存在になった。漫画は、世の人々に世界に目を向け**させる**一手段になり得るという信念は、手塚の遺産の一つである。

■M.D. 医学博士　■have little to do with ～にほとんど関係のない　■comic strip コマ割り漫画　■prolific 多作の、精力的な　■long-running 長期の　■break new ground 新境地を開く　■convince ～ to … ～を…させる

参考文献
References

Gessel, Van C., Three Modern Novelist: Soseki, Tanizaki, Kawabata. Tokyo: Kodansha International, 1993.

Hane, Mikiso, and Louis G. Perez, Modern Japan: A Historical Survey, Fifth edition. Boulder, Colorado: Westview Press, 2013.

Hunter, Janet E., Concise Dictionary of Modern Japanese History. Berkeley: University of California Press, 1984.

Jansen, Marius B., The Making of Modern Japan. Cambridge and London: The Belknap Press of Harvard University Press, 2000.

Jansen, Marius B., Sakamoto Ryoma and the Meiji Restoration. New York: Columbia University Press, 1995.

Japan: An Illustrated Encyclopedia. Tokyo: Kodansha Ltd., 1993.

Kasahara Kazuo (ed.), A History of Japanese Religion. Translated by Paul McCarthy and Gaynor Sekimori. Tokyo: Kosei Publishing Company, 2001.

Kashiwahara Yusen and Sonoda Koyu (eds.), Shapers of Japanese Buddhism. Translated by Gaynor Sekimori. Tokyo: Kosei Publishing Co., 1994.

Kato Shuichi, A History of Japanese Literature: The Years of Isolation. Translated by Don Sanderson. Tokyo: Kodansha International, 1983.

Keene, Donald. World Within Walls: Japanese Literature of the Pre-Modern Era, 1600-1867. New York: Henry Hold, 1976.

Kitaoka Shinichi, Self-Respect and Independence of Mind. Translated by James M. Vardaman. Tokyo: Japan Publishing Industry Foundation for Culture, 2017.

Kornicki, Peter, The Book in Japan: A Cultural History from the Beginnings to the Nineteenth Century. Honolulu: University of Hawai'i Press, 2001.

Miner, Earl, Hiroko Odagiri and Robert E. Morrell (eds.), The Princeton Companion to Classical Japanese Literature. Princeton: Princeton University Press, 1985.

Morris, Ivan, The Nobility of Failure: Tragic Heroes in the History of Japan. Fukuoka, Japan: Kurodahan, 2013.

Murakami Hyoe and Thomas J. Harper (eds.), Great Historical Figures of Japan. Tokyo: Japan Culture Institute, 1978.

Rimer, J. Thomas, A Reader's Guide to Japanese Literature. Tokyo: Kodansha International, 1988.

Rimer, J. Thomas (ed.), Mori Ogai: Youth and Other Stories. Honolulu: University of Hawai'i Press, 1994.

Sachiya Hiro, Hiro Sachiya Talks About Japanese Religion. Translated by James M. Vardaman. Tokyo: Japan Book, 2010.

Starr, S. Frederick, Inventing New Orleans: Writings of Lafcadio Hearn. Oxford, Mississippi: University Press of Mississippi, 2001.

Time Magazine, 60 Years of Asian Heroes. November 13, 2006.

Totman, Conrad. A History of Japan, second edition. Oxford: Blackwell Publishing, 2005.

Varley, Paul, Japanese Culture, fourth edition. Honolulu: University of Hawai'i Press, 2000.

著者

ジェームス・M・バーダマン
James M. Vardaman

1947年、アメリカ、テネシー州生まれ。プリンストン神学校、修士、ハワイ大学アジア研究専攻、修士。早稲田大学名誉教授。著書に、『シンプルな英語で話す日本史』『シンプルな英語で話すアメリカ史』『シンプルな英語で話す西洋の天才たち―Western Genius』(ジャパンタイムズ出版)、『英語で話す「仏教」Q&A』(講談社バイリンガル・ブックス)、『外国人によく聞かれる日本の宗教』『日本現代史』(IBCパブリッシング)、『地図で読むアメリカ』『毎日の英文法』『毎日の英単語』(朝日新聞出版)、『アメリカの小学生が学ぶ歴史教科書』(ジャパンブック)、『アメリカ南部』(講談社現代新書)、『黒人差別とアメリカ公民運動』(集英社新書)、『アメリカ黒人史―奴隷制からBLMまで』『英語の処方箋』(ちくま新書)など多数ある。

訳者(日本語訳)

長尾 実佐子(ながお みさこ)

翻訳業。主に海外ニュースや雑誌記事の翻訳に従事するかたわら、英語学習書、ビジネス書、自己啓発書等の編集者としても活躍中。著書に『魔法の口ぐせ　ビジネス英語』(共著　明日香出版社)、訳書に『日本人が絶対間違える英語大全』『ネイティブがよく使う英会話フレーズ400』、『マナー違反な英会話』(KADOKAWA)などがある。

イラスト:飯村俊一　　組版:キャップス　　編集協力:細田繁

日英対訳　世界に紹介したい日本の100人

2021年4月15日　第1版第1刷印刷
2021年4月25日　第1版第1刷発行

著者　　ジェームス・M・バーダマン
訳者　　長尾　実佐子
発行者　野澤武史
発行所　株式会社山川出版社
　　　　東京都千代田区内神田1-13-13　〒101-0047
　　　　電話　03(3293)8131（営業）
　　　　　　　03(3293)1802（編集）
印刷　株式会社太平印刷社
製本　株式会社ブロケード
装丁・デザイン　黒岩二三［Fomalhaut］

https://www.yamakawa.co.jp/

©2021 Printed in Japan　ISBN 978-4-634-15189-5